"Hold on to your h[...] us on a journey through a realm ruled by monstrous women and hungry dinosaurs. In *Clever Girl*, McGregor offers a queer feminist reading of *Jurassic Park* that celebrates the wild, the ravenous, and the rageful while honoring the kinship and care we need in our apocalypse survival kits."

— Zena Sharman, author of *The Care We Dream Of*

"*Clever Girl* lives up to its title, bringing us a witty, sharp, and deeply moving take on *Jurassic Park* — a movie easily dismissed as box-office schlock. Hannah McGregor cracks open its feminist utopian potential and reminds us that nothing is disposable when you try to make your way through the end of the world."

— Karen Tongson, author of *Normporn: Queer Viewers and the TV That Soothes Us*

"Almost a lifetime after *Jurassic Park* was released, my sister and I still practice 'creepwalking' around the kitchen — tipped toes, hands up, wide eyes, bared teeth. If you dig velociraptors, you'll love watching sassy scholar Hannah McGregor systematically dismantle a '90s classic with her queer-feminist lens. If you love reading smart books, you'll appreciate this artful dance of storytelling and cultural criticism."

— Chantal Gibson, author of *with/holding* and *How She Read*

"Fans of *Jurassic Park* will love this close reading, which creates fully realized orchestral songs from all the promising queer, feminist, and decolonial bells the movie rings in our minds. *Clever Girl* is attentive and open, engaging a depth of academic research alongside lively prose that moves at a quick clip."

— andrea bennett, author of *Like a Boy but Not a Boy*

"This is the dinosaur book I didn't know I needed. Hannah McGregor unpacks the queer refusals that the dinosaurs embody in the original film and not only offers us ways to re-imagine our relationships with the monstrous parts of ourselves but encourages us to re-think how we understand kinship, community, and collective meaning-making in this era of crisis and transformation. Read it now!"

— Zoe Todd, Fish Philosopher

"It's a joy to watch Hannah McGregor examine the film like a prism, with each rotation revealing a new flash of intimate memoir, brilliant feminist analysis, and apocalypse survival guide."

— Tajja Isen, author of *Some of My Best Friends*

the pop classics series

clever girl.

jurassic park

hannah mcgregor

ecwpress

Published by ECW Press
665 Gerrard St. East
Toronto, Ontario, Canada M4M 1Y2
416-694-3348 / info@ecwpress.com

Editor for the press: Jen Sookfong Lee
Copy editor: Jen Knoch
Cover and text design: David Gee

Library and Archives Canada Cataloguing
in Publication

Title: Clever girl. Jurassic Park / Hannah
McGregor.

Other titles: Jurassic Park

Names: McGregor, Hannah, author.

Series: Pop classic series ; #14.

Description: Series statement: Pop classic
series ; #14

Identifiers: Canadiana (print) 20240354591 |
Canadiana (ebook) 20240354605

ISBN 978-1-77041-739-7 (softcover)
ISBN 978-1-77852-287-1 (PDF)
ISBN 978-1-77852-284-0 (ePub)

Subjects: LCSH: Jurassic Park (Motion picture)
| LCSH: Feminist films.

Classification: LCC PN1997.J833 M36
2024 | DDC 791.43/72—dc23

Printing: Friesens   5 4 3 2 1
PRINTED AND BOUND IN CANADA

This book is funded in part by the Government of Canada. Ce livre est financé en partie par
le gouvernement du Canada. We also acknowledge the support of the Government of Ontario
through the Ontario Book Publishing Tax Credit, and through Ontario Creates.

ECW Press is a proudly independent,
Canadian-owned book publisher. Find
out how we make our books better at
ecwpress.com/about-our-books

The interior of this book is printed
on Sustana EnviroBook™, which is
made from 100% recycled fibres and
processed chlorine-free.

MIX
Paper | Supporting
responsible forestry
FSC® C016245

For all the
fat femmes,
clever girls,
and
monstrous mommies

"Their existence gives the lie to the thought that the wild is always something untouched by human hearts and hands. The wild can be human work."

— Helen Macdonald, *H Is for Hawk*

"This in the end is what matters, not that we stand proudly in all our monstrousness every day, but that we find small ways to gestate dissent and deviation, to nurse and nurture the things that are supposed to be wrong with us, until they grow into something great — this is our strength. That each of us has the capacity not only to be a monster, but a mother of monsters. We can birth from our own bodies every one of men's fears."

— Jess Zimmerman, *Women and Other Monsters*

"FEMME SHARKS DON'T EAT OUR OWN. FEMME SHARKS LIKE TO EAT THOUGH."

— Leah Lakshmi Piepzna-Samarasinha, "FEMME SHARK MANIFESTO!"

Contents

Introduction

"Objects in mirror are closer than they appear": On Looking at Dinosaurs and Dinosaurs Looking Back

The first glimpse of a dinosaur we see in Steven Spielberg's 1993 blockbuster *Jurassic Park* is just an eye, glaring through the bars of a cage, coldly intelligent and filled with an otherworldly hunger. We don't see another dinosaur for almost 20 minutes, but that eye haunts the rest of the film. It hovers in our thoughts, watching us as we watch the dinosaurs, reminding us that they are not only props nor exhibits but something else altogether, something simultaneously sentient and caged and furious.

I was nine years old when I first saw *Jurassic Park* in a theater, and even by that age, my obsession with dinosaurs was well underway. There was plenty fueling that flame — a seemingly endless and capitalistic supply of dinosaur toys and children's books — but the initial spark was the fossil gallery at the Canadian Museum of Nature. Amongst the dusty dioramas of Ontario wetlands and cases and cases of rocks and minerals, the dinosaur fossils were a shock to my childhood senses. I had seen real-life birds and rocks before; dinosaurs belonged to another world altogether. Part of my awe was at their sheer enormity, their fossilized skeletons looming over me despite my size; I was always big for my age, broad and sturdy and tall, graceless next to other girls. But the Museum of Nature didn't just stick a skeleton in a room with a plaque — they went all-in on evoking the strangeness of the world dinosaurs lived in, decorating the displays with enormous ferns and piping in an imagined soundscape of ancient jungle noises.

Staring up at those fossils, I was transported to a world so different from my own that I swear I could feel myself disappear; something in my chest cracked open and let the infinite in. A couple of years later, sitting in a darkened theater, feeling the *thump-thump-thump* of the T. rex's footsteps vibrate in my chest, I felt that sensation again. If I'd known this word back then, I would have called my encounters with dinosaurs "sublime." Their vastness made me feel small, not in the ways that, as a girl, I was already accustomed to feeling small — sneered at by the cool kids, picked last for every team — but in the way the ocean or a really tall mountain can shock me with a sudden awareness of my own insignificance. In the face of the sublime, I become at once nothing and everything, part of the majestic and meaningless stuff of creation.

Neither oceans nor mountains were in my aesthetic vocabulary at the time; the landscape of Eastern Ontario was less sublime vistas and more of the aforementioned rocks and birds. I grew up in a tiny postwar house on a one-block dead-end street in the decidedly provincial town that was Ottawa in the late '80s and early '90s. I was one of two children in a straight white Protestant household, surrounded by other children being raised in other straight, white, Protestant households. My world was small, though I mostly didn't realize that because it was all I knew. Summer vacations were cabins or camping or some combination of the two, surrounded by other white families that looked a whole lot like mine. We visited lakes usually — never one of the imposing Great Lakes with their oceanic tides and ship-swallowing storms, mind you, but one of the thousands of small lakes that dot Eastern Ontario, sludgy little bodies of water bordered by cattails and populated by snapping turtles and schools of tiny brown and silver fish flickering in the shadows, lakes you wanted to avoid the edges of because the murky bottoms threatened leeches. Better to canoe out to where it was deeper and jump in from there. These spaces didn't feel any wilder, to me, than my own backyard, thick with ferns and hostas, echinacea and bee balm, sage and mint and two kinds of parsley.

If you grew up in a big city, this might sound quite adventurous to you. But like all aesthetic categories, the sublime is a matter of perspective, a function of familiarity and personal experience.

Our imaginations, writes nature writer Verlyn Klinkenborg in his article "What Were Dinosaurs For?," "tend to normalize the strangeness of nature, and . . . one of the immense virtues of science is its unceasing ability to defamiliarize what we thought we knew." Encountered first in museums and later in classrooms, dinosaurs were a shock to my system, hinting at a world so much larger than what I had seen. They tugged at my imagination with the promise of something more — more chaotic, more unruly, even, dare I say, more *queer*.

THE MONSTROUS ~~GAYS~~ GAZE

Why do we love looking at dinosaurs?

Jurassic Park is a film about looking, but as feminist film scholar Laura Mulvey has argued, so are most films. Within the visual language of cinema, the camera operates like an eye through which we, as viewers, might enjoy our scopophilia — literally the pleasure of looking — without being ourselves subject to the gaze. And as Mulvey explains, that cinematic gaze has traditionally been a deeply gendered one, enacting a masculine pleasure in looking at objectified women. We can slot *Jurassic Park* into this same tradition: it's a film about the pleasure of looking at dinosaurs, and those dinosaurs are (not coincidentally) all female, and all being actively objectified as professional showman John Hammond and his team of scientists attempt to turn them into spectacles.

Jurassic Park was a technological and cinematic breakthrough, winning the 1994 Academy Award for Best Visual Effects. It also marked the apex of a long history of people vying to secure the rights to display dinosaur remains. Fossil-hunter Barnum Brown, who discovered the first T. rex remains in the early 20th century, was funded by the American Museum of Natural History: he was looking for fossils specifically to put them on display. Scholar Lisa DeTora, writing about the Chicago Field Museum's acquisition of the famed T. rex fossil nicknamed "Sue," argues that this purchase was really about "ensuring that she would be available to the public gaze in perpetuity."

That desire to possess and display the remains of dinosaurs is part of a longer history of crowd-pleasing spectacle dating back to the earliest forms of American popular culture, a history ironically evoked by Barnum Brown's name; his parents named him after famed circus showman P.T. Barnum. Perhaps you're familiar with P.T. Barnum from the 2017 musical *The Greatest Showman*, a shockingly bad film that recasts him as a champion of the underdog, when in reality he perpetuated a series of hoaxes grounded in exploiting non-normative bodies. Barnum got his start by touring and displaying an enslaved Black woman. Her name was Joice Heth, and he claimed that she was 161 years old and had been "mammy" to George Washington himself. When his audience grew bored with her, Barnum planted a rumor that Heth was, in fact, a convincing automaton, "made up of whalebone, India-rubber, and numberless springs ingeniously put together."

Joice Heth reminds us that the origin of American popular culture, and its fascination with staring at technological marvels, is entangled with the display of gendered and racialized bodies. As scholar Louis Chude-Sokei has argued in his article "The Uncanny History of Minstrels and Machines, 1835–1923," Barnum's claim that Heth was an automaton is entangled in the "history of freakery, ethnographic display, and the complex birth of both the museum and the Western carnival-circus complex." As museums and circuses — parallel institutions of popular spectacle — sought out ever more exciting exhibits, they also helped to demarcate the boundary between the human and the not-quite-human, those who were counted as subjects and those who could be displayed as objects of curiosity. Joice Heth was already dehumanized by being toured as a curiosity, and Barnum's later claim that she was an automaton furthered that dehumanization, pushing her deeper into the category of *thing* rather than *person*.

Both P.T. Barnum's circus and Barnum Brown's fossil hunting were in service of a public hungry for something exciting to look at, and who were fascinated by new technologies that might be able to trick them into mistaking fantasy for reality. Dinosaurs — at once real and surreal, natural and constructed by the paleontologists whose job it was to piece their skeletons back together — scratched that voyeuristic itch. And that's the same itch that John Hammond, the fictional creator of *Jurassic Park*'s fictional park, is targeting.

Hammond is a kind of modern-day P.T. Barnum, calling for us to step right up, tricking us with artifice while promising to show us something real, something we can see and touch. Hammond calls that "an aim not devoid of merit," and we're invited to sit in the question of that merit: yes, people could die, but even if they do, they will get to look at dinosaurs first. By evoking Barnum and the history of the circus, the film also evokes the violence of that history and the horrifying complicity that comes from gazing upon something — or someone — that you are being told is yours to look at, an ownership of voyeurism.

Bear with me for a moment here: we need to talk about the relationship between knowledge and power. At the heart of white supremacy is the belief that white people are not only the natural leaders of civilization, but also that we are uniquely qualified to divvy the rest of the world up into categories and hierarchies and then to produce knowledge about them, knowledge that naturalizes those invented categories. The invention of race as part of the project of colonialism, for example, allowed 19th-century scientists to then develop pseudoscientific techniques like phrenology — the study of human skull shape as an indicator of intelligence and moral character — that produced knowledge about racial identity. These new scientific "truths" were in turn legitimized by institutions like universities and medical schools, further dividing the world into those who produced knowledge and those who knowledge was produced *about*. Spectacles, we must conclude, are always entangled in questions of power — the power of who is looking and of how they name what they're looking at.

At the heart of the success of *Jurassic Park* was how beautifully it produced in viewers the sense that the dinosaurs were real and really there. Spielberg used both cutting-edge computer-generated visuals from Industrial Light & Magic, as well as life-sized animatronics. When the dinosaurs get close, when our protagonists touch them, they feel real because they are — because they're actually there, beautifully wrought machines, not of whalebone and India-rubber but certainly numerous parts ingeniously put together. As John Hammond welcomes his visitors to Jurassic Park, he welcomes us as well: when Drs. Grant and Sattler — the scientists whose approval he needs — first look at the dinosaurs, we look, too, and alongside them we are swept up in the sheer joy of looking. John Williams's majestic score washes over us, underlining that what we are seeing is larger than life, that it is sublime. But we are also swept into these parallel histories of circuses displaying non-normative bodies for entertainment and films displaying female bodies for the male gaze.

What particularly thrills Grant and Sattler, though, is the experience of looking at a *real* dinosaur rather than a representation of one. As they look, they breathlessly exchange their new scientific certainties — that brachiosaurs are warm-blooded, that they move in herds — and invite us to share in the joy of unmediated contact, despite the fact that *our* contact is, in fact, extremely mediated, not only through the film itself but also through the many representations through which we encounter dinosaurs *in* the film. Whether it's goofy didactic videos or reflections in mirrors, *Jurassic Park* encourages us to look but never lets us stop thinking about our own looking and about the technologies that have shaped it. "Objects in the mirror are closer than they appear" reads the warning on the jeep mirror as our heroes narrowly escape a lunging T. rex. The dinosaurs might *appear* to be right there, on a screen so close that we could touch it, but the dinosaurs themselves are still out of reach.

In their kitchen showdown, Hammond's grandchildren Lex and Tim escape the raptors by outsmarting them with reflections — the raptors don't know what a mirror is (yet). In part we, the audience, are safe because, like our protagonists in those moments, we're never actually looking right at the dinosaurs: we are always seeing them through layers of film-making, a movie-made looking glass that reminds us again and again that these are not real dinosaurs but representations that come from human minds. And because they come from human minds, they have been distorted and misidentified by what we expect them to look like, by the desires we bring into our experience of looking. As any true dinosaur nerd will tell you, *Jurassic Park*'s clever girls are not even velociraptors; they're actually deinonychus (from the Greek for "terrible claw") and were deliberately misnamed by Michael Crichton, the original novel's author, because "velociraptor" is more fun to say and most Americans don't have a working knowledge of Greek.

The dinosaur renaissance was already well underway when *Jurassic Park* was released. The discovery of new fossils in the 1960s and '70s had led paleontologists to theorize dinosaurs as intelligent, warm-blooded, and active rather than cold-blooded behemoths inevitably wiped out by their own sluggishness. These discoveries had reinvigorated public interest in dinosaurs, and *Jurassic Park* threw about $914 million of fuel on that fire (that's the worldwide gross of the opening run), shaping a generation's understanding of dinosaurs. Don't believe me? Just google "Was T. rex's vision motion-based?" It absolutely was not; they probably had excellent vision, considering the size of their orbital cavities (those are the eyeholes in the skull, for the uninitiated) and besides they probably hunted using mainly smell. That made-up fact, introduced by Dr. Grant as he saves Lex and Tim from the movie's T. rex, was based on the screenwriter, David Koepp, misunderstanding a detail in Crichton's novel. The T. rex had flawed vision because of the way she'd been genetically engineered. The franchise doubled down on this error of adaptation, obsessed with the cinematic possibilities of having to lie very, very still while a T. rex snuffles over your body like a horse looking for a sugar cube.

Like renaming deinonychus "velociraptor," depicting dinosaurs as scaled, and creating their distinctive roars, making the T. rex's vision motion-based was a creative liberty; that so many of these liberties continue to shape popular understandings of dinosaurs is a reminder of the outsized cultural impact this film has. They also underline the refractory quality of *Jurassic Park*. The film not only encourages us to gaze at dinosaurs but alters our very perceptions of what we're gazing at, mirroring how the scientists in Hammond's labs alter the dinosaurs they're cloning to make them more controllable. In this sense, the dinosaurs are constantly subject to the objectifying force of the human gaze. There's nothing they can do to stop us from looking.

But there's also nothing we can do to stop them from looking back.

I am a fat, queer, heavily tattooed, facially pierced, and at the moment of writing this, teal-haired woman. All of which is to say: I'm used to being looked at. If, like me, you are a non-normatively-bodied person, if you are visibly disabled or fat or a person of color, if you are someone whose body is marked by difference from the culturally defined ideal, then you have experienced the weight of the world's gaze upon you. In an airport recently, I felt that gaze grow heavier than usual, like a hand resting on my shoulder, pinning me down. I didn't know what was drawing it — my fatness, my queerness, the mask I was wearing in a crowd of unmasked people — but its presence was both unmistakable and unnerving. Not sure how to respond, I opened Twitter and wrote a joke about it, about the not-knowing; in response, friends suggested that these strangers were probably looking at me because I looked so cool. Their reassurances rang hollow. If you're used to being watched, you know that weight intimately. And you might also know that one of the most effective ways to respond is to meet the watcher's eye.

Jurassic Park isn't just about the display of dinosaurs: it's about the *failure* of that display, the refusal of the dinosaurs to be reduced to stops on a tour or exhibits in a museum. This messaging is ironic, considering that when the film hit theaters in 1993, it not only *didn't* fail but achieved an unprecedented level of success. The viewers didn't get eaten, which meant that they could go back and see it again, and the merchandising wasn't a wry nod to capitalism's overreach but rather part of what made *Jurassic Park* such a hit. Its level of success was literally unprecedented: it broke multiple records, for opening weekend, number of days it took to hit $100 million and then $200 million, and then for being the first movie to surpass $500 million worldwide. And while a "black swan event" like this is never fully reproducible — by definition, it's an event that happens by surprise, has unpredictable results, and can't be recreated — *Jurassic Park*'s runaway success sent Hollywood a clear message: audiences were excited about the larger-than-life cinematic possibilities of computer-generated special effects. As a nine-year-old viewer, though, I may have taken a different message home with me.

If there's a reason *Jurassic Park* has stuck like a burr to our culture, it's not Sam Neill's charming neckerchief or Laura Dern's khaki shorts or even Jeff Goldblum's open shirt and glistening chest: it's the dinosaurs, brought to life on the screen for us, sneezing and flocking and stomping and roaring, shaking our very sense of human supremacy. For all its pseudoscientific trappings, *Jurassic Park* isn't really about what dinosaurs *were*; it's about how they can make us — the viewers, and the characters whose awe and terror we get to experience vicariously — *feel*. "When Dinosaurs Ruled the Earth" reads the banner that flutters across a roaring T. rex in the film's climax. That "when" is 100 million years ago but also, somehow, right now.

In the years that followed my first viewing of *Jurassic Park*, I would have ample opportunities to learn, again and again, those first lessons that looking at dinosaurs had taught me: that the world was so much bigger and older and stranger than I had ever imagined, and that humans can attempt to control that strangeness only at our own peril. My mother would get sick, and then die, thrusting me into a world without safety or assurances. I would come to realize I was queer, and then that I was asexual, upending any neat ideas I had about the contours that a life might have.

Throughout these changes, the dinosaurs have accompanied me, acquiring new layers of meaning as I grew, their monstrosity, like all new things, gradually shifting from the sublime into the familiar, until one day I realized that rather than fearing these enormous creatures, I had come to identify with them. I, too, have felt caged and furious. I, too, have figured out how to make kin for myself despite being told that I could not. And I, too, have wanted to devour the architects of a world that could not contain me. Coming face to face with the sublime beauty and terror of life itself, I have learned how to look it in the eye, unblinking.

1

"Clever girl": The Queer Erotics and Feminist Monstrosity of Velociraptors

In 1993, the media landscape for a nascent feminist was, let's say, *sparse*. I remember my mother's concern about the models of femininity I was being exposed to: Barbies and Disney princesses primarily, and without any of the attention to diversity those brands have incorporated in recent years. My mother was worried about my exposure to feminist role models for a few reasons. She was a feminist herself, hairy-legged and braless, deeply committed to refusing the norms of femininity that had been forced on her in her own childhood; she gave me a copy of *Our Bodies, Ourselves*, eager to share the women's liberation she had encountered throughout the '70s. But also, and this is key, I was a fat kid. Neither of my parents had been fat kids, and my brother was as lanky as them, so I was a bit of a mystery, a throwback to the sturdy Mennonite farm women of my mom's side of the family, perhaps. I wish I could say that my mother was a fierce defender of my body as it was, but body positivity hadn't gone mainstream in the '90s, and she didn't have a vocabulary for helping me to understand my fatness as anything but profoundly unacceptable. So she went looking for those possibilities, in artwork of ancient fertility goddesses and huge warrior women, and she worried when all I wanted to do was play with Barbies and pretend to be Ariel every time I got in a pool.

I recall her, one evening when I was around 14, leaning over my shoulder to look at the comic I was reading — *Gen13*, a series about five sexy superpowered teens. (So sorry, I just realized through some googling that there was a *Gen13* movie released in 2000; I'll be back in one hour and twenty-six minutes. Update: it's okay.) "That's an unrealistic representation of women's bodies," she told me. "Real women don't look like that." I rolled my eyes. I *knew* real women didn't look like that, but I was 14 and horny and closeted and I wanted to look at drawings of tits. I didn't say any of that out loud, of course. Bodies were a touchy subject between us, anyway; I knew she wanted me to lose weight, that she was worried about my health, genuinely, because neither of us had heard of "health at every size" and because she was dying and felt an urgency around mothering me. She wouldn't be around for much longer, didn't feel like she had the time to waste with letting me figure myself out. She wanted me to lose weight, and she wanted me to know that women's bodies didn't have to look like they did in comics, that, in fact, they *couldn't* look like that. It was a lesson I couldn't hear at the time, the bodies I looked at too tangled up in my teenaged hormones, my shame and desire and confusion.

But what other models did I have? Where could I see women whose bodies looked like mine, women taking up space? Fat women tended to be plump-breasted caretaking types, but even by nine I was already resentful of that trope. Taller and bigger than all my classmates, I was immediately thrust into a fat-mommy role, told by friends and family and teachers at school that I was a natural nurturer, that it was my job to look after my smaller and more delicate friends and classmates. I have spent much of the rest of my life aggressively refusing this stereotype and its concomitant demands for emotional labor. But if I wasn't going to rest children's heads on my pillowy breasts, then who was I? After I watched *Jurassic Park*, I realized I had another option before me, and that was to become monstrous.

WHAT ACTUALLY HAPPENS (IN CASE YOU FORGOT)

Here's a detail of *Jurassic Park* you may have forgotten: all of the dinosaurs are engineered to be female to prevent them from reproducing. Is this detail a mere curiosity, or is it — bear with me here — the entire point of the movie?

Jurassic Park is an adaptation of Michael Crichton's best-selling 1990 novel, a thriller-cum-cautionary tale responding to the emerging science of genetic engineering. The novel has a lot more granular detail about the engineering of the dinosaurs and the process's unpredictable results, but the movie simplifies the whole thing down to an explanatory video and a few passing lines of dialogue. As the outrageously Southern-accented talking DNA strand explains, Jurassic Park's scientists recreated "*dyno-sours*" by extracting "dino DNA" from mosquitos preserved in amber, sequencing the genome, and then filling in the gaps with DNA from frogs. The frog DNA is the technical explanation for why the dinosaurs end up being able to reproduce; as Dr. Grant explains, some species of frog can change sex to reproduce in same-sex environments. In the novel, I understand, there is much more to be said about lysine and dichogamy and migration patterns, but the movie keeps things fairly straightforward: the dinosaurs were engineered to all be female in order to control their reproduction, and that attempt at control failed. As professional skeptic Dr. Malcolm put it: life, uh, found a way.

Here are a few more key plot points, again, just in case you've forgotten. But seriously, just go watch the movie; it slaps. Jurassic Park (the park *in* the movie) is the creation of ultra-wealthy tech CEO John Hammond (Richard Attenborough), about whom we know a small handful of things: he's Scottish, he dresses entirely in white, he hates lawyers, and the first attraction he ever created was a flea circus. Hammond is in the business of attractions — we know he also has a game reserve in Kenya, an aside that firmly roots him in the history of colonialism — and Jurassic Park is set to be his most exciting and successful one yet, if he can keep the lawyers, and the investors they represent, from shutting it down. The investors are upset because an employee got eaten at the beginning of the movie, and they're not convinced that more employees *won't* get eaten, which is very bad for insurance and liability purposes. Their lawyer Donald Gennaro, played in classic weaselly lawyer fashion by Martin Ferrero, tells Hammond that if some respected scientists will sign off on the park, then the investors will be satisfied, which is honestly as much a fantasy as bringing dinosaurs to life. Imagine a world where large corporations respect the word of someone with a PhD.

Anyway, Hammond and Gennaro gather up their scientists and, ill-advisedly, Hammond's grandchildren and, even more ill-advisedly, send the majority of the park's employees away for the weekend so that everyone remaining can get nice and familiar with the park's untested attractions, including its miraculous computer-automated systems that for sure aren't going to shut down. Enter paleontologist Dr. Alan Grant (Sam Neill), paleobotanist Dr. Ellie Sattler (Laura Dern), and "chaotician" (that's a mathematician specializing in chaos theory) Dr. Ian Malcolm (Jeff Goldblum). They meet on the helicopter traveling to the fictional Isla Nublar, off the west coast of Costa Rica, and it quickly becomes clear to everyone involved that Jeff Goldblum is going to be the runaway charismatic star of the entire movie. In a moment of delightfully on-the-nose foreshadowing, Dr. Grant finds that his seatbelt only consists of two buckles, the *female* ends of the belt (get it? they're female, like the dinosaurs), and like life, Grant finds a way: he knots the two female ends together. Hold on to that detail, because much of my argument about the dinosaurs' queerness hinges on this moment.

Grant and Sattler are initially blown away by the viscerally powerful experience of seeing actual real live dinosaurs. They're our audience surrogates in those early encounters, and their wonder is our wonder. But that means that as they start getting suspicious about how well thought through the park actually is, their concern also becomes our concern. When Dr. Malcolm warns Hammond's lead scientist Dr. Henry Wu (played by a criminally underused B.D. Wong) that the kind of control they're attempting can only ever be a fantasy in complex systems, Wu smirks back at him: "You're saying this group of female animals will breed?" No, Malcolm replies, even though he is kind of saying that; maybe he just doesn't want anyone to laugh at him for not understanding how reproduction works. Grant isn't paying attention, too busy focusing on the realization that *the park is breeding velociraptors*. This is very bad because, as game warden Robert Muldoon (played by Bob Peck dressed up like a sexy Steve Irwin) confirms, velociraptors love murder.

Later that day, Grant and Sattler and Malcolm set out on the park's maiden tour/voyage, accompanied by Gennaro as well as Hammond's grandchildren, hacker Lex (Ariana Richards) and dinosaur nerd Tim (Joseph Mazzello). The tour is supervised from a blue-lit command center by Hammond and Muldoon alongside Ray Arnold (Samuel L. Jackson), the park's chief engineer, and Dennis Nedry (Wayne Knight), the park's programmer. What follows is a cascade of system failures, symbolic of the chaos theory that Malcolm just so happens to be an expert in. His examples of chaos begin with a drop of water rolling off Dr. Sattler's hand and escalate to all the dinosaurs breaking free and doing a variety of unpredictable things, like reproducing despite all being female (in your face, Dr. Wu) or eating the lawyer. When our surviving protagonists eventually reunite, they are finally ready to put aside their differences and agree that, actually, breeding dinosaurs was a pretty bad idea.

We've got lots of time to get into chaos theory, complex ecologies, and big-tech morality tales, but at its core this movie is about humans thinking we can control nature and being proven wrong. The form that nature takes is female animals who subvert control in every conceivable way: by bursting out of their enclosures, forming hunting packs, and, of course, breeding. The breeding is thematically important, for sure. It is life finding a way, it is control failing, and more subtextually, it is the patriarchal fantasy of women as perfectly malleable and perfectly controllable falling apart.

The capacity for all-female societies to reproduce is a recurring motif in feminist utopias; in Charlotte Perkins Gilman's 1915 novel, *Herland*, for example, women reproduce through parthenogenesis, eliminating the need for men altogether. Parthenogenesis is not what's happening in *Jurassic Park*: the process Dr. Grant describes, called dichogamy, is common in flowers, fish, snails, and other intersex organisms, allowing them to cross-fertilize. Scientifically, this means that the dinosaurs are all intersex, but the film insists on their femaleness.

The ability to reproduce is something that has been denied them — that's the language Dr. Wu uses, "deny" — and like their freedom and their ability to hunt, it is something they violently reclaim. Remember that moment when Grant ties the two female ends of his seatbelt together? He doesn't find some clever way to turn one of the buckles into a tongue, just like half the dinosaurs don't suddenly become male. No, Grant circumvents the whole tongue-in-buckle logic by making a knot, a symbolic rejection of a binary and heteronormative logic in which only the male and female — the buckle and the tongue — can fit together. And that knot, like the engineered dinosaurs of Jurassic Park, is decidedly queer.

VELOCIRAPTORS ARE SEXY

My favorite entry in *The Toast's* now-discontinued "If X Were Your Y" essay series is Michelle Vider's "If the Velociraptor from *Jurassic Park* Were Your Girlfriend." In it, Vider unfurls the queer erotic undertones of the all-female dinosaurs, specifically the largest and most vicious of the three velociraptors: "Her head rests above yours, her legs behind yours, her tail curled around both of you, her wrist and those claws, *those claws*, resting against your stomach." Okay, maybe you aren't convinced that a potential disemboweling is erotic, but the subtext is there throughout the movie, from Grant slowly running a velociraptor claw across a horrified child's belly to Muldoon murmuring "Clever girl" right before he's oh-so-cleverly eaten.

The velociraptors hold a special place in the imagination of the movie, and that's because they held a special place in the origins of the story. Crichton was in part inspired by reading the work of paleontologist John Ostrom, whose discovery of the fossilized remains of the deinonychus in the late 1960s spurred what has been referred to as the "dinosaur renaissance." Ostrom is the one who argued that dinosaurs had evolved into birds (a stance attributed to Grant in the movie), and deinonychus's sleek, bird-like body and raptor claws likely had something to do with that. A new generation of paleontologists like Ostrom and Robert Bakker (whom Tim namechecks in the movie as having written a book longer than Dr. Grant's) transformed both the study of dinosaurs and the popular understanding of them by demonstrating that they hadn't been cold-blooded, lumbering evolutionary failures, but warm-blooded, intelligent, and adaptable. Once we came to understand that dinosaurs could be agile predators, intelligent pack hunters with complex social dynamics, then all of a sudden we wanted to talk about them again. Perhaps it is man's eternal struggle to see an incredibly deadly animal and think, "I want to know everything about that," which might just be code for "I could fight that."

Fascination with the deadliness and intelligence of velociraptors dominates the entire franchise. By *Jurassic Park III*, the raptors are having full conversations with each other in clicks and warbles, tracking humans through the jungle to retrieve their stolen eggs, and being described by Grant as possessing human levels of intelligence; by *Jurassic World*, they've got names and personalities and an inexplicable fondness for Chris Pratt.[1] But in the original, their intelligence is pure malevolence. The other dinosaurs, even the enormous and deadly T. rex, are animals; if you understand them well enough, you can survive them, if not outright control them. Sure, T. rex is huge and loud and will totally eat you, but unlike the raptors, she isn't associated with monstrosity or a malevolent feminine hunger. While the velociraptors are repeatedly referred to as female, the T. rex is mostly called "he" and framed in terms of majesty and instinct rather than cruelty or malice.

But the velociraptors are not comprehensible, controllable, or survivable. Their most insidious feature is their capacity to learn, beginning with testing the electric fences on their enclosure and escalating to their mastery of doorknobs. T. rex hunts because she's hungry; the velociraptors hunt because they want *you*, specifically, to die. Their behavior cannot be explained by animal instinct. There's no way they're still hungry after eating Muldoon *and* Arnold, and yet they stalk the film's protagonists unrelentingly, right up until our beautiful T. rex intervenes. They're smart, they're determined, they love to murder, and they're female.

---

1 There are currently six movies in the franchise as a whole: *Jurassic Park* (1993), *The Lost World: Jurassic Park* (1997), *Jurassic Park III* (2001), *Jurassic World* (2015), *Jurassic World: Fallen Kingdom* (2018), and *Jurassic World Dominion* (2022). All six movies take place in the same world and share continuity, with characters reappearing between films (Dr. Malcolm, for example, appears in *Jurassic Park*, *The Lost World*, *Fallen Kingdom*, and *Jurassic World Dominion*). Critics generally agree that the franchise is of steadily deteriorating quality, though I'll admit a fondness for *Jurassic World Dominion* because it features the return of Laura Dern as Dr. Sattler and she wears a really cool vest.

The concept of the monstrous feminine comes from feminist film scholar Barbara Creed's book appropriately titled *The Monstrous-Feminine*, which demonstrates how cinematic visions of monstrosity so frequently draw on female reproductive functions, from the perverse mothering of vampires siring other vampires to the vagina-dentata-esque design of the aliens in *Alien*. The monstrous feminine is not merely a reversal of male monsters, a gender-swapped Dracula or a ghost that happens to be a girl; no, the monstrous feminine is monstrous *because of* and *through* its femininity, rooted in Western culture's deep and pervasive horror of bodies that can menstruate, get pregnant, and give birth; bodies that are penetrable and that leak various fluids; bodies that are permeable and messy. I know what that horror feels like, both from other people — a man recoiling in instinctive disgust when I mention I'm menstruating, say — and toward myself, as I wash blood out of my clothes in a restaurant bathroom. That horror is written large on movie screens throughout the history of cinema. Chances are if you see a gaping maw full of sharp teeth and a wet, dark interior, that maw is telling you something about the Western horror of vaginas and their dark secrets.

I saw just such a maw recently, visiting a museum exhibit about the T. rex, who is always, always depicted with her mouth open. In a darkened room at the Telus World of Science in Vancouver, I stood next to a life-sized reproduction of a T. rex, her body thrust forward over powerful hind legs, head lunging toward the ground as though she had just spotted prey (*you are that prey* was the spine-chilling subtext), mouth open, strings of saliva connecting razor-sharp teeth, lights angled just so to cast a perfect shadow of those teeth onto the ground below. Those insistently displayed teeth — that endure despite recent and unsettling studies suggesting tyrannosaurs probably had lips — insist that T. rex's function is first and foremost to devour. She is, as one exhibit panel put it, "built to kill."

In *Women and Other Monsters*, Jess Zimmerman lists the many ways in which women can become monstrous: by being too sexy or not sexy enough, too hungry or ambitious, too angry, too large. She advocates not only for us to understand how monstrosity has been constructed, but to actively embrace it, to *become* monstrous. There's a term for the subversive embracing of historically maligned traits: it's called radical negativity, and it's an approach to culture practiced by a lot of minoritized communities, particularly queer, trans, racialized, and disabled folks. When we cannot find ourselves reflected in the heroes and protagonists of stories, we instead learn to see ourselves in the villains, especially in properties where villains tend to be queer-coded. Look no further than Ursula the Sea Witch from Disney's animated classic *The Little Mermaid*, a high-femme octopus witch modeled on the drag queen Divine, the most memorable star of John Waters's camp films. Ursula has become a cherished icon for fat women and queer folks — see, for example, Tituss Burgess's iconic cover of Ursula's signature song, "Poor Unfortunate Souls"[2] — not despite but *because* of her villainy, her monstrosity.

It is only as an adult that I've come to realize how *Jurassic Park*'s monstrous dinosaur-women, alongside figures like Ursula and the harpy in *The Last Unicorn* (more about her in a moment), introduced me to visions of monstrous femininity that shaped my own queerness and feminism. Fat, closeted, and deeply uncomfortable in my own skin, I spent my youth trying to make myself smaller while admiring these onscreen versions of women who were unabashedly enormous and powerful, and whose monstrosity freed them from the regime of heterosexual desirability. The dinosaurs were an early lesson in the fact that I, too, could be enormous, loud, and deadly, if I wanted to be.

Of course, as a fat kid, I was absolutely not going to tell my friends or classmates that I identified with dinosaurs — they already made enough jokes about me sitting on them or eating them — but these monstrous women unlocked a longing in me.

Before I fell in love with *Jurassic Park*, my favorite movie was the eerie '70s animated classic *The Last Unicorn*, adapted from the novel by Peter S. Beagle. This story of an evil king capturing all the world's unicorns is a parable about capitalist greed and environmental extraction, as well as a compelling metaphor for menstruation ("Now that I'm a woman, everything has changed," sings the unicorn before she goes to confront the "red bull" . . .). Despite her metaphorical function

---

2 Do yourself a favor and go watch this. It's on YouTube at https://youtu.be/1mz6tw5Zddg.

as a symbol of purity and its loss, the unicorn is also a kind of monster, a throwback to a world of magic that humans no longer believe in. In the midst of her travels, the unicorn is captured by Mommy Fortuna, a witch who uses her powers of illusion to disguise mundane animals as magical creatures and display them in a dingy traveling carnival, in yet another invocation of the history of circuses caging and displaying so-called monstrous bodies. Easily seeing through Mommy Fortuna's cheap magic, the unicorn identifies the one other creature that is real: the terrible, ancient, and immortal harpy Celaeno. Mommy Fortuna knows that Celaeno will kill her one day, but her inevitable death is worth it because, however briefly, she has put the unspeakable wildness of the whole ancient Earth in a cage. She will die, but Celaeno will not, and "she will remember forever that *I* caught her, and *I* held her prisoner. So there's my immortality, eh?" The harpy's monstrosity is more clearly on display than the unicorn's — she is horrible, huge and beaked and many-breasted — but she and the unicorn are sisters in immortality, fossils of a strange world. They are, both of them, dinosaurs.

As a child, I was awkward in my body, more harpy than unicorn. I was tall and big for my age, with bad hand-eye coordination and a wincing fear of pain that my mother eventually routed out of me through horseback riding lessons, where my size and strength could become an asset rather than a hindrance. Because I was big and chubby, children and adults alike attributed my lack of physical graces to a wrongness in my body. I was always too much, too big, too loud, too strong. I had a clumsy, puppy-like desire to play with my friends and a tendency to accidentally hurt them; other girls were so small, so dainty, so quick to cry. The only time I can recall my size not being a problem was in fifth grade when the kids in my class were into playing horse-and-rider. I made a good horse.

My too big body was also read as a kind of gender failure. I couldn't dress cutely, doomed to frumpy adult clothes by 12. I had breasts early, but the girls in my third grade class made sure I knew it was only because I was fat. To make matters worse, I was a very girly girl. I liked tutus and Barbies and unicorns and stationery; I wanted to be a pretty princess and was aware that I was not and probably never would be. And so, around the edges of my love for all things pink and frilly, a shadow began to grow, and that shadow was a fascination with monsters.

The monsters that drew me had three things in common: they were big, they were angry, and they were women. Ursula, Celaeno, and of course my beloved dinosaurs, the T. rex especially, so big, so hungry, so frustrated by her enclosure. Though my body felt like a cage, I had a nascent understanding, years from articulation, that I could be free if the circumstances were different, that I was only a monster because the people around me kept telling me I was. I longed for permission to be enormous and devastating, not yet realizing that our own enormity is something we must claim, often violently. Monsters, after all, do not ask permission.

I've referred to the dinosaurs in *Jurassic Park* as monsters, or at least as monstrous, a few times now. But their monstrosity — the way they can be read as monstrous women, as the boogeyman of a horror story — lives alongside their animality. When Lex, traumatized by almost being eaten, shies away from a brachiosaurus, screaming, "Don't let the monsters come over here," Grant corrects her: "They're not monsters, Lex. They're just animals." That "just" speaks volumes: if they're animals they can be tamed, understood, managed. Animals are natural and thus comprehensible; monsters are unnatural, but not in the way we define civilization as unnatural, as moving away from the blood and fury of nature into something safer and more contained. The monstrous has also moved away from the natural but in the opposite direction, becoming not more civilized but more uncontrollable and more existentially threatening. Animals can be tamed, but monsters must be destroyed.

The question of nature versus monstrosity is mostly subtext rather than text in *Jurassic Park*. The dinosaurs are framed narratively as wild animals who are out of place and time, confused and hungry and just acting the way animals will. The notable exception is the velociraptors, who are associated with a malignant, quasi-human level of intelligence, tipping into the monstrous because of that intelligence. They aren't just reacting to stimuli, they're learning, and they use what they learn to try to eat children. But dig a little deeper and we can see that all of the dinosaurs are monstrous in the sense that they are unnatural, genetically altered for the purposes of the park to be incapable of breeding and to die without medical interventions. And those are only the intentional consequences of their genetic hybridity, before we add on T. rex's strange vision or the dinosaurs' ability to change sex. The malleability of the dinosaurs, their chaotic capacity to escape the grasp of masculine science and Western rationality, is the crux of their monstrosity. This is, after all, what female monstrosity does: it makes a mockery of attempts to control or even fully understand it, like the unfilmable witch in *The Blair Witch Project* or the sexy but unkillable alien hybrid in *Species* or basically every movie in the *Alien* franchise. It's tempting to then say that *Jurassic Park* is a movie horrified with the monstrous feminine, seeking to tame and control women's unruly bodies.

The problem with that reading is that everyone fucking *loves* these dinosaurs. Even the raptors are praised for what they are: "Clever girl," Muldoon says right before he's presumably disemboweled by one of those iconic toe claws. Of the many utopian possibilities offered by this film — a society of all women, a violent takedown of technocapitalism and extractive tourism — perhaps the one that holds my imagination tightest is the idea that monstrous women may be praised not despite but precisely for our monstrosity. That someone might be so captivated by the majesty of you disemboweling your prey that they just can't look away. That they might look you in the eye as you slide a claw into their gut and say, "Good job."

This is also the queerest thing about the movie for me, Laura Dern aside. Because it's in queer community that I first found this thrilling possibility made real: my loudness, my fatness, my ferocity, all the things that made me too much, were suddenly not only accepted but celebrated. Rather than subtly suggesting diets or exercise regimes, or asking me to state my opinions less forcefully because I'm being "intimidating," my friends now give me pins that say "fat babe" or just "bitch." At my 39th birthday party, one guest lovingly described me as having the energy of that one friend who wants you to poison your husband (or, as another friend put it, referring to the iconic murder ballad by The Chicks, I'm "serving 'Goodbye Earl'"). I could be that lead velociraptor, the big one, eating park employees and testing electrical fences, and someone would look at me and say, "I am terrified of you, and you are magnificent." Never mind that if a man ever condescendingly called me a "clever girl," I might actually be moved to disembowelment.

Arguably the scariest thing the dinosaurs do, though, isn't end life but create it. Despite being a movie entirely devoid of human mothers, *Jurassic Park* is extremely concerned with dinosaur procreation. The dinosaurs might well be put in the category of giant sci-fi women that Emily Yoshida writes about in "Do Androids Dream of Colossal Women?" Yoshida is writing about *Blade Runner 2049* and links the fixation on giant women to the film's obsession with motherhood and biological reproduction. We might make a similar extrapolation about *Jurassic Park*: the dinosaurs — at least, some of them — have become literal monstrous mothers, rendered all the more monstrous and uncontrollable through the fact of their motherhood. But rather than being erotically charged, big, sexy mommies that you might Freudishly climb back inside of, the dinosaurs are going to drag you back into the womb kicking and screaming via the gnashing orifices of their many-toothed mouths.

That image is . . . well, it's not *not* erotic, let me put it that way. But it's also queerly erotic, decentring heteronormative understandings of sexuality as penetrative and reproductive in favor of erotics as the evocation and celebration of all that is wild and joyful and powerful within us. That's the understanding at the root of Vider's piece on dating the velociraptor: the wildness and untamed monstrosity of the velociraptor calls to *your* wildness and monstrosity. You do not tame her with your love; instead, you "go with her into the wild," just as the protagonists in *Jurassic Park* must embrace wildness to survive (an image encapsulated for me in a sweaty and blood-stained Laura Dern sprinting through the jungle).

There's no implication here that you're fucking the raptor. What's erotic is the proximity to her danger, the awareness that she could kill you at any moment and does not . . . for now. It's an erotics of the sublime, the visceral thrill of realizing how small and helpless and insignificant you are, and it hovers under the surface of so many of the human interactions with dinosaurs that we see throughout *Jurassic Park*: Dr. Sattler weeping as she touches a sick triceratops, Lex hesitantly reaching out to commune with a brachiosaurus before getting coated head to toe in dinosaur snot (there's a subtext there that I don't particularly want to dive into; feel free to unpack it on your own time). Even the way Dr. Grant holds his breath as the T. rex snuffles ever closer to him, practically undressing him with her heavy breath, suggests a frisson of something thrilling within the terror of this proximity. To be close to a dinosaur is to be close to something so viscerally other that it brings your own animality to the surface.

FEMME SHARKS AND QUEER DINOSAURS

I've been grappling with the gender of dinosaurs, but that's only appropriate because I've been grappling with my own gender as well. Years after I finally came out, first to myself and then gradually to my community, as queer, I experienced a second coming out, as asexual. Recognizing and naming my own asexuality has been a fraught multi year experience. I first heard the term in 2014 or 2015, the gentle offering of a queer friend to whom I had just tearfully confessed that I feared I was broken because I couldn't make myself want anyone. My fatness and queerness had given me a complicated relationship to my own desirability, one that for years had stood in the way of conversations about the possible substance of that desire. I was too busy worrying about being wanted to ask what I might want for myself. As I began to dig into that question, I couldn't believe that the answer might be: no one. Deeper than the fear of an unfamiliar sexual orientation, though, was the conviction that asexuality was a one-way trip to profound loneliness. I had spent much of my 20s watching friends enter relationships and immediately stop having time for their friendships; this was something they framed to me as inevitable, even as part of the process of "growing up." Now I was picturing a future in which everyone else gradually paired up and I was left behind, alone.

In the years since, this fear has been allayed, not because I was wrong but because I have deliberately fostered queer community in which friendship is not placed hierarchically below romantic relationships, in which I am valued and celebrated as a queer auntie and beloved friend. Part of my conviction that I am both queer and asexual lies in the fact that queer community is the place where my asexuality is seen and celebrated, whereas within the discourses of reproductive heterosexuality, I am a failure. I suppose my asexuality is another kind of monstrosity that I've found celebrated in queer community, like my fatness, my loudness, the too-muchness of my ferocity and my love. And lately, when I look at my fat, queer body in a mirror, I've begun to ask: am I a woman? Does the category or concept of woman mean anything to me? Is the gender failure of my fat body perhaps its own kind of exciting queer possibility?

In lieu of thinking of myself as a woman, I've been increasingly thinking of myself as a femme. "Femme" is a queer term that embraces and reclaims many of the stigmatized qualities of femininity, including community care and emotional labor, without linking it to essentialized characteristics of womanhood or the binary logics of heterosexuality. And while work on femme politics and ethics often focuses on questions of care, there is also space in femme community for monsters. Look no further than writer and disability justice activist Leah Lakshmi Piepzna-Samarasinha's "FEMME SHARK MANIFESTO!" i.e., my favorite manifesto of all time. Femme sharks embody not the meekness and delicacy of femininity as defined in a patriarchal framework, but rather a femininity that is ravenous, loud, and unruly: "FEMMES ARE [. . .] REVOLUTIONARIES DEDICATED TO TAKING THE SYSTEM THE HELL DOWN SO WE CAN BE FREE!" Femme sharks "THINK EATING A BIG-ASS MEAL IS SEXY"; they "HAVE BIG MOUTHS AND . . . KNOW HOW TO USE THEM"; they are "TOUGH" and "HUNGRY" and "FIERCE."

This is the female monstrosity I find in *Jurassic Park*. The dinosaurs are monstrous women, and they are femme sharks. They are ravenous, they are loud, they are committed to taking down the system of the park so that they can be free. The fact that we don't know their biological sex, that they defy the attempt of the scientists to control their sex as a means of controlling them, only underlines their queerness, evoking the history (and current day battle) of trans and intersex people fighting against these same forms of control by a white supremacist and patriarchal medical system that strives to violently reinforce a culturally constructed sex/gender binary. I don't want to undermine the gender play of these intersex dinosaurs by insisting that they're all women, even as their proximity to woman-ness is central to their monstrosity.

Fat, femme, queer, hungry, monstrous, full of rage, and determined to be free: no wonder I have gravitated to these creatures as feminist role models. They offer a fantasy of freedom that sparked a young girl's imagination, and since then has grown into a full-on obsession with what is possible when we embrace, without fear or shame, sublime monstrosity.

2

"Life, uh, finds a way": Settler Colonialism, Dinosaur Ecology, and the Violence of Discovery

The Lost World — the celebrity-studded 1997 follow-up to *Jurassic Park* — is a very silly movie that I mostly refuse to acknowledge because it recasts Dr. Ian Malcolm as a hypermasculine action hero, which entirely misses the point of both the character and Jeff Goldblum. But it does have one perfect line of dialogue, when Malcolm is called to Hammond's sickbed and learns that Jurassic Park has been rebranded as a nature preserve. "So you went from capitalist to naturalist in just four years," Malcolm says. "That's something." He's not praising Hammond here; if anything, he's expressing some well-earned skepticism about Hammond's intentions, which is literally always a good thing to do, because eat the rich. (Truly: eat the rich before they eat you, or genetically engineer some dinosaurs that then eat you.) No, what Malcolm is saying is that Hammond's nature preserve is just a rebranded theme park, another iteration of Hammond attempting to control nature by exerting his will, an action that is absolutely going to blow up in his face — or more accurately, in the faces of his employees.

Back when I taught English to engineering students, there was an essay I really enjoyed discussing with them. It was about restoration ecology — the attempt to restore equilibrium in an ecosystem that has been disrupted by human intervention — and it asked the question: is it better, once humans have ruined something, for us to keep interfering in the hopes that we can fix it again, or should we just leave it alone and let nature take its course? The former tends to be hubristic, because most human intervention emerges from a Western scientific perspective that fails to properly account for the complexity of systems, but the latter is dangerous, because nature taking its course doesn't always work out well for us. On the one hand, human intervention into complex systems is frequently an extraordinarily bad idea; on the other hand, we can't make decisions about ecosystems as though we aren't also part of them. What happens to our ecosystems happens to us because, as much as we might like to forget it, we are also animals.

A HEALTHY FEAR OF NATURE

I live in Vancouver, a city where we are getting a front-row seat for the human-engineered climate crisis. Every year, the forests catch fire. We call it a good year when they don't catch fire too much, though the "too much" depends on who you're asking. In Vancouver, we tend to ignore the fires until the smoke arrives, making the air unbreathable and turning the sun a portentous dark red; if you're living in Kamloops or Nelson your experience of the fires is more visceral than a front-row seat: you're an actor on the stage. In the summer of 2021, British Columbia was hit with a "heat dome," a natural event made devastatingly worse by the effects of climate change, resulting in record-breaking temperature highs and the full-scale destruction of the town of Lytton, home of the Lytton First Nation. In Vancouver, hundreds of people died from heat exposure, with ambulances delayed by hours as they sought to respond to an unprecedented number of calls. We didn't build our cities for these kinds of temperatures, and while there are laws in Canada governing how cold your apartment is allowed to get, there are not yet laws governing how hot it can be, meaning landlords have no obligation to provide their tenants with — or even *allow* them — air conditioners. We're beginning to learn what people in other parts of the world have known for a long time: you can die of heat as easily as you can die of cold.

There are countless cultural, economic, historical, and political causes behind climate change, but entangled in all of these reasons is a fundamentally Western hubris: we believe we have control over nature. Look, for example, at the history of cultural burns in the Okanagan region. Prior to colonizers arriving and taking control of the landscape, the Okanagan was carefully and deliberately stewarded via practices including the burning away of brush and the controlled burning of landscapes to maintain wildlife habitats and help ecological cycles. These traditional practices of land management were rooted not in an attempt to control or violently transform the landscape, but in an understanding of humans as part of the ecosystem and thus as vital contributors to it.

The concept of the ecosystem is a relatively recent one, coined by English botanist Sir Arthur Tansley in 1935; a pioneer in the field of ecology, or the study of how living organisms relate to each other, Tansley proposed the idea of the ecosystem as a way of understanding that living organisms are inseparable from their environments. The transfer of energy between living organisms and their environment (think of the lion dying and feeding the earth which grows grass which feeds the zebra which then feeds the lion — yes, I learned ecology from *The Lion King*) means that you can't add or remove any component of an ecosystem without disrupting its entire finely tuned equilibrium. The complexity of ecosystems is part of what makes restoration ecology such a tricky topic, and unsurprisingly the biggest restoration ecology successes have been led by First Nations with tens of thousands of years of sophisticated understanding of how ecosystems function as compared to Western science's not-quite century — again, look at the example of cultural burning. The genocidal violence of colonization disrupted these fire practices through the relocation of First Nations and the decimation of their populations and later through explicit legal prohibitions against cultural burns. In Vancouver, we see the effects of colonization in action every summer, as the smoke darkens the skies and fills our lungs.

Jurassic Park takes place almost entirely on Isla Nublar, which, as a reminder, is a fictional island off the coast of the nonfictional Costa Rica. As far as the movie is concerned, it was an unoccupied island prior to Hammond selecting it for his bad, bad park. It's always a good idea to be suspicious when some white men look at a place and say, "Wow, look at this totally untouched landscape where absolutely no one lives, I guess it's mine now." The concept of terra nullius, or "nobody's land," was based on the colonial assertion that there is "nobody" present, which, according to the doctrine of discovery, allows explorers to claim the land for their own countries if it is currently unoccupied. Of course, "nobody" isn't literal; it's a political category. Unoccupied land only had to be unoccupied by Christians, meaning that Christopher Columbus, for example, could claim the Americas as unoccupied territory despite the presence of hundreds of millions of Indigenous people.

Despite the evocative similarities between "nullius" and "nublar," "Isla Nublar" actually means "cloud island" in Latin, likely making it a fictional stand-in for Isla del Coco, which is hundreds of kilometers off the coast of Costa Rica and is known for its cloud forests, a kind of rainforest that only occurs in rare circumstances of elevation and moisture conditions, alongside its 70 endemic flowering species and 65 endemic insect species. "Endemic" means that they occur only there — because Isla del

Coco was never physically connected to a continent, it's full of endemic species, a completely unique site of biodiversity that in the real world is carefully protected from human intervention.

In *Jurassic Park*, though, it is a blank slate for the imposition of a new order, one that claims to be natural when it's anything but.

Okay, let's pause here and talk about nature for a moment, shall we? It's a tricky term, with a ton of connotations and cultural baggage. Is it the opposite of civilization — that which humanity hasn't intervened in — or is it the opposite of the unnatural, something that is innate or inherent in the world? Is nature a pristine landscape untouched by human presence, or is it whatever homophobes think straight marriage is? In *Jurassic Park*, nature is a sentient force, sometimes used interchangeably with "life," to indicate the complex systems that humans cannot fully comprehend or control: nature as ecosystem. And in a lot of ways, *Jurassic Park* and its many sequels are classic "man versus nature" movies. Did you learn about those narrative divisions in high school? Man versus nature, man versus man, man versus self, etc.? Man versus nature is almost always about an encounter with the sublime, whether that's represented by a white whale or a mountain that someone is determined to climb. I have a fondness for these kinds of stories because they so often circle around the problem of supposed human supremacy: we think we're in charge right up until we get a good look at the natural world, and then we suddenly remember how very small we are. That or we plant a flag in it.

I hate the politics of most of the movies in the *Jurassic* franchise — they're conservative, heteronormative, and super racist — and similar critiques could be leveled at *Jurassic Park*. We could think about the role of the family across Spielberg's oeuvre, for example, or about the fact that Laura Dern was 23 when she filmed it to Sam Neill's 42, which tells us a lot about what we expect adult women to look like. It doesn't pass the Bechdel test unless you count the velociraptors clicking to each other about eating Lex and Tim (which I might), and there are awfully few women involved in any aspect of the production. But I didn't watch this movie in the context of its sequels, its director, or its politics of production. I encountered it as a kind of fairy tale or modern myth, one that had allegorical lessons to teach me about the world and my place within it. Alongside *The Last Unicorn* (message: don't put unicorns, or harpies, into cages), it formed part of the backbone of my moral education. Message: don't get so caught up in seeing if you can that you forget to consider if you should. Also, you should have a healthy fear of nature. That is exactly where Hammond — and his lawyers, scientists, and everyone else who thinks dinosaurs can be controlled — goes wrong: they just should have been more scared.

I certainly grew up with such a fear, though whether it was healthy is a matter of perspective. We were a camping-and-backwoods-cabins kind of family — I mean the kind of cabins with no electricity and no running water and an outhouse in the back stocked with 15-year-old magazines. My parents were dyed-in-the-wool hippies with a great belief in the value of children spending time in nature: breathing fresh air, entertaining ourselves without TV, and getting properly dirty. I was a squeamish little fussbucket of a kid, but I still had to learn to put a worm on a hook and gut a fish, how to build a fire and dig a hole to poop in. We also learned what was worth being afraid of. Snakes, for example, weren't a problem: in Eastern Ontario they were almost guaranteed to be garter snakes, which are harmless if not outright adorable. In my 20s, I invited a friend from England to visit me in Ottawa, and I quickly learned that what I considered to be a run-of-the-mill level of outdoorsiness was, for someone raised in central London, basically a parody of the Canadian-as-lumberjack. They thought I was joking when I first suggested going for a canoe ride, and when I attempted to delight them, one morning, by showing them all the garter snakes sleeping in the mulch pile in my parents' garden, they screamed like the dozens of tiny snakes were a full-sized T. rex.

The first moose I ever saw was on a family vacation to Nova Scotia. I was nine and my brother twelve, and it would be our last camping trip because it turns out that teenage boys don't do well trapped in a tent with their little sisters. In retrospect, I'm pretty sure I was an annoying little sister; my brother was authority-resistant and rebellious from day one, constantly pushing against boundaries, whereas I was an anxiously well-behaved child. Our mom's illness only pushed both of us further in these directions, and further away from each other. So we were probably squabbling in the backseat that night, as my dad drove the family minivan along a narrow and winding road, trees looming blackly on our right and a cliff falling away to our left. As we rounded a corner it was there, enormous and antlered and alien in the moonlight, standing across both lanes, staring us down. My fear was immediate and visceral: this animal was the size of our minivan and it could kill us so easily, and worse yet, it had every right to do so, because we were in its home. When it wouldn't move on its own, my dad began to honk the horn and flash the headlights. From the backseat, I begged him not to, certain that it would respond by bashing us straight off the road into the abyss.

It didn't. Eventually it ran back into the woods and we kept driving, but a moose, I am still convinced, is an awful lot like a dinosaur, a scion of an ancient world shaped by neither benevolence nor animosity but by sheer animal indifference. When you see something like that, what is your reaction? Do you want to touch it, interact with it, befriend it? Tame it even, *own* it, to remind yourself you are more powerful somehow? That desire to lock wild animals up for the pleasure of human interaction is alien to me; I'd much rather leave them alone, a preference I attribute to a lifetime of respectful fear. Without that fear, people can do some pretty messed up things like, say, build a theme park full of murder-minded dinosaurs.

OOPS, I'M ABOUT TO COMPARE DINOSAURS TO LITERATURE

The message that nature is sacred and awe-inspiring and also will totally eat you feels like a particularly Canadian moral, and whole generations of Canadian writers and literary critics would agree. The early literature written by white settlers has often been about an enormous and unsympathetic wilderness that might be kept at bay but can never be fully conquered. Famed literary critic Northrop Frye called it the "garrison mentality," that sense that settlers are walled in together in a fort on the edge of civilization, and beyond those walls are things that want to eat us or at the very least freeze us to death. My favorite example is Earle Birney's 1951 poem "Bushed," in which a man goes mad because a mountain looks at him funny.

It perhaps goes without saying but let me say it anyway: this is a profoundly colonial attitude. The world cannot be neatly divided into nature and civilization, the wild and the tamed or, as French structuralist Claude Lévi-Strauss put it, the raw and the cooked. What is currently known as Canada was not an untouched wilderness when settlers arrived but the home of hundreds of nations who had spent tens of thousands of years stewarding and caring for the land and their other-than-human kin. Plus, you know, we *are* animals, as much as we like to deny it. Dinosaurs know the truth: for all our civilization, we're still made of meat.

But there's something that really tickles me about that settler terror of what lies beyond the edges of the clearing. Never have I experienced that macabre delight more than when, at the age of 20, I visited Sir John Franklin's memorial in Westminster Abbey. Franklin was a British Royal Navy officer who, in 1845, tried to sail through the Northwest Passage, a route the British were hoping would expedite trade with Asia. The ships got frozen in the ice and the whole crew was lost, meaning that memorial doesn't contain his remains. Instead, it is marked by a verse written for him by then poet laureate Alfred, Lord Tennyson that begins "Not here: the white north has thy bones." The frisson of emotion I experienced in that moment had nothing to do with the heroic sailor and his tragic death; I identified, immediately and viscerally, with the icy landscape hungry for British bones. This identification has, as part of its origin, my ferocious love of dinosaurs and for all things monstrous and hungry and sublime.

My comparison of the unyielding bone-hungry north to a dinosaur has its own literary precedents. In E.J. Pratt's *Towards the Last Spike*, a 1952 long poem about building the Canadian Pacific Railway, Pratt imagines the Canadian Shield as a giant lizard who, like the "white north," had an appetite for settler skeletons: "She'd claim their bones as her possessive right / And wrap them cold in her pre-Cambrian folds." In Pratt's poem, the heroic railway-builders overcome the distinctly dinosaur-esque landscape, a blatant elision of the hundreds of Chinese workers who died in that four-year span, their absence famously pointed out in F.R. Scott's 1968 response poem/diss track "All the Spikes but the Last." Rereading *Towards the Last Spike*, though, I can't help but imagine that pre-Cambrian dino rearing back and consuming the white men who, in their hubris, thought to drive spikes into her majestic hide, leaving the shattered ribs of the railways as a memorial to their failure and the triumph of the wild. In fact, I would prefer all stories of white male heroism to end in failed dreams, shattered infrastructure, and memorials reading "not here."

Which is, of course, why I love *Jurassic Park* so much: it doesn't end in the triumph of completed infrastructure but in the shattering defeat of Hammond who, dressed all in white like a joke about a colonizer, gives his beloved park one last mournful look before departing forever. Nature has won, right? Well, sort of. Because whatever ecosystem existed on Isla Nublar prior to the introduction of dinosaurs and long-extinct prehistoric plants, you better believe that it has been, let's say, *disrupted*. Hammond may have failed, but he's done irreparable damage to Isla Nublar and by extension to the surrounding ecosystems that Isla Nublar interacts with, because it turns out some dinosaurs can fly and some dinosaurs can swim and some dinosaurs get removed from their island sanctuary by power-hungry capitalists. As Malcolm puts it, "If there is one thing the history of evolution has taught us it's that life will not be contained. Life breaks free, it expands to new territories and crashes through barriers, painfully, maybe even dangerously, but, uh . . . well, there it is."

There it is indeed: the articulation of something almost like a critique of colonialism. Jeff Goldblum's iconic Dr. Ian Malcolm, "chaotician," has the dual role of being the movie's unlikely sex symbol and its forewarner. But, alongside Dr. Sattler (who quickly points out that the park is an ecological disaster, mixing and matching plants and animal species from completely different eras), Dr. Malcolm serves another role: he models a decolonial critique of Western science, including attention to the unpredictable messiness of complex systems and resistance to arrogant human interventions. He advocates for "humility before nature" and condemns profit-motivated scientific advancement. In this sense, we can read *Jurassic Park* through not only a feminist but also a postcolonial lens. Through that lens, we can see the film's critique of the horrors of colonization — as both a process and a way of relating to the world as inherently comprehensible and controllable — and we can also notice the absences that structure the film, particularly the violence being wrought on the other-than-human kin whose home Hammond and his scientists have invaded to create their truly terrible park.

A striking real-world parallel to Hammond's treatment of dinosaurs is the extraction of fossil fuels. In "Fossil Fuels and Fossil Kin," Métis anthropologist Zoe Todd comes to the realization not only that dinosaurs "would . . . have enacted forms of kinship with one another, but that by living on top of their resting place, I too held responsibilities to honour their resting place and, perhaps, to consider my own relational obligations to them." The mining, heating, fracking, shipping, and burning of these fossils, Todd concludes, "seems a rather violent way to treat kin." Todd's recognition, which echoes through *Jurassic Park*, is this: if you understand yourself not as the owner of nature but as a part of it, deeply entwined in complex and more-than-human kinship relations, then you treat nature very differently.

Métis writer Warren Cariou's 2012 short story "An Athabasca Story" encapsulates the clash of extractive colonial worldviews with Indigenous relational ones. In it, Elder Brother goes looking for a place to warm himself but can't find any of his relations; instead, he finds the Athabasca tar sands, the center of crude oil extraction in Alberta. Rebuffed by the workers he meets there, who threaten to lock him up for trying to steal the valuable resources the company is extracting, Elder Brother reflects that these men talk "as if [they] had no relations at all" and decides that if they won't share with him, he'll take some of the dirt for himself. As he reaches into the earth, though, a voice responds, "Elder Brother, you're hurting me!" Consumed by greed, Elder Brother digs deeper and deeper until he finds himself "stuck fast in that Athabasca tar." "Help me!" he calls out to the voice he heard before. "I'm sorry I didn't listen to you." But the voice is silent, and stuck fast in the tar, Elder Brother is extracted "as if he was a fossil" and made into fuel himself. By failing to treat the earth itself as his relation, Elder Brother dooms himself to the same fate: dehumanized, commodified, and burned for profit.

MOVING FAST AND BREAKING THINGS

A few years ago, I introduced a feminist friend to *Jurassic Park* (a role I play in many feminists' lives, since they tend to assume that it's a dude movie, for dudes). At the end, she summarized it as "what happens when you move fast and break things," alluding to the foundational ethos of Silicon Valley or any other high capitalist project of extraction and exploitation. Jurassic Park — the park itself, not the movie — presents a utopian fantasy of total human control, one that is entangled with how humans so often think of ourselves as the end (meaning both the final stage and the goal) of history. Rooted in this worldview is a kind of ahistorical imagination, a scientific presentism that cannot learn from the past because it does not acknowledge it — a viewpoint that has more than once led to the senseless loss of life. Look, for example, at the implosion of the *Titan* submersible in June 2023, a fully preventable tragedy driven by corporate greed and billionaire hubris that eerily echoes the story of the *Titanic*, whose shipwrecked remains the *Titan*'s passengers were trying to visit. In the wake of the disaster, emails were unearthed from OceanGate CEO Stockton Rush — who died aboard the *Titan* — in which he complained about safety standing in the way of innovation.

Dr. Malcolm summarizes this cavalier attitude toward scientific progress in his famous condemnation of Hammond's team: "Your scientists were so preoccupied with whether or not they could, they didn't stop to think if they should." The "should" there is an ethical question, and like most ethical questions, it implies the ability to learn from past mistakes to make future decisions and to *slow down* in the face of discovery.

If Hammond and his team of scientists — specifically Dr. Wu, who as the sole Asian character gestures to the techno-orientalism of many Western dystopias — are standing in for tech culture's insistent presentism, our paleontological heroes model a different kind of knowledge, one that is slow, cautious, and curious. As a trained scholar in the humanities, I'm used to grouping tech and science together as "those people over there who are getting funding," but science as a pursuit of knowledge for knowledge's sake has much more in common with the slow and intentional work of archival research than it does with the tech ethos of disruption and rule breaking.

Methodologically speaking, much of science is, in fact, characterized by its slowness. At the heart of scientific knowledge is the premise of reproducibility: if you do a study or an experiment, someone else should be able to redo the same experiment and get the same results. Repetition is essential to this approach, as is a reliance on precedent and understanding of the past that so rarely comes through in how we equate science with innovation and newness. That slow thinking about the past is, of course, most evident in scientific fields that engage with the past itself, like geology and paleontology, explorations of a world so long gone that it almost defies human imagination.

It matters that Dr. Alan Grant is, in the words of Juanito Rostagno — the proprietor of the amber mine where they're finding all those dino-blood-filled mosquitos — "a digger." The digging we see Grant involved in is a slow and painstaking process, clearing debris off a fossil to avoid damaging it and panicking when Hammond arrives in a freaking helicopter like a real billionaire asshole and blows dust all over the dig site. This tactile learning is contrasted, from the beginning, with the intertwined forces of technology and capitalism. Dr. Grant and technology don't get along, and he is inherently skeptical of innovation for innovation's sake. He and Dr. Sattler agree to serve as experts for Hammond's park not because they're excited to see what he's come up with, but because he promises to fund their dig for an additional three years, a reminder that scientific discovery is profoundly intertwined with capitalism. These scientists can, to a certain extent, be bought, and it's clear that Hammond expects them to be "his" experts: he's outraged when they express suspicion over the safety of the park, because they're supposed to be on his side.

The ideal of scientific objectivity would tell us that science isn't on anyone's side; in reality, that kind of true neutrality can exist only in a vacuum where science isn't being done by and for people but somehow, purely, for itself. The history of American paleontology is littered with millionaires like Andrew Carnegie and J.P. Morgan, philanthrocapitalists seeking to secure symbolic capital by funding fossil digs and the subsequent displays of these fossils, all the while building their fortunes through land theft and resource extraction. As historian of science Lukas Rieppel has argued, museums incorporated vertical integration strategies that allowed them to control fossils from discovery through to display in a way that mirrored the growth of American corporations in the Gilded Age. Contemporary museums go to great lengths to distance themselves from what nature writer Verlyn Klinkenborg calls "the Barnum-like hustle of their dime-museum predecessors," but Hammond's blithe collapsing of flea circus and scientific innovation, of discovery and display, reminds us how closely intertwined they've always been. Looking at dinosaurs is indivisible from the history of museums, which in turn is indivisible from the history of

American spectacle. And when Hammond brings Grant and Sattler to Isla Nublar, he's counting on them being so swept up by the experience of looking at the dinosaurs that they'll set their objections aside.

Instead, they turn a skeptical gaze on everything around them, wrenching themselves out of the role of spectator and breaking through the veneer of the park to understand how it actually works. First they force their way out of the educational ride Hammond straps them into, literally shoving away the bars holding them in place and inserting themselves into the labs they were only meant to look at through glass. Then on the disappointing jeep tour — disappointing because the dinosaurs don't show up on command — they leave the jeeps behind to walk into the jungle and interact with a sick triceratops. Our protagonists are constantly asking questions: they don't just want to gaze passively at the remarkable fact of the dinosaurs, but insist on digging deeper, understanding how they were made and how they're interacting with their new ecosystems including, in the case of the sick triceratops, eating plants they shouldn't be eating. When Dr. Sattler plunges her arm into an enormous mound of dinosaur droppings, she's telling us something important about her tenacity — her literal willingness to get in the shit and to relate in intimate and messy ways with the dinosaurs she's been brought in to observe from afar. Sattler and Grant don't move fast and break things; they go slow and work toward repair and understanding.

The most obvious foil to this ethos is not Hammond himself but computer programmer Dennis Nedry, played by the unrelentingly charismatic Wayne Knight, who uses his control of the park's systems to engage in a little light corporate espionage. Specifically, he's selling dinosaur embryos to Hammond's rival at a bioengineering company called Biosyn (you can tell they're the bad guys because they have the word "sin" in their company's name). Nedry promises Dr. Lewis Dodgson that by shutting down the park's security systems for 18 minutes, he'll let Biosyn catch up on 10 years of research.

That, the film wants us to know, is *too fast*, and nothing good comes of speeding toward discovery without pausing to consider the consequences. This is how Malcolm articulates his philosophical opposition to what Hammond and his scientists have done at the park:

I'll tell you the problem with the scientific power that you're using here: it didn't require any discipline to attain it. You read what others had done, and you took the next step. You didn't earn the knowledge for yourselves, so you don't take any responsibility for it. You stood on the shoulders of geniuses to accomplish something as fast as you could, and before you even knew what you had, you patented it and packaged it and slapped it on a plastic lunch box, and now you're selling it, you want to sell it!

He might as well be speaking directly to those fast-moving Silicon Valley bros who created the Facebook "Like" button or Twitter's retweet function, many of whom have since publicly stated their regret for the social implications of these technologies, like former Google employee Tristan Harris warning us that "a handful of tech companies control billions of minds every day." This phenomenon is so widespread that education writer Audrey Watters has termed it "the Tech 'Regret' Industry." The general thesis of these statements of regret is that innovation for innovation's sake is both violent and irresponsible, even if what it achieves is miraculous.

And they have, it is clear, gone too fast at Jurassic Park. Hammond brags over and over that they "spared no expense," but he's always talking about the tourism side of the park, like the quality of the ice cream or the celebrity voice actor guiding the tours. When it comes to the safety of the park itself, they have, in fact, spared *some* expense, particularly via Nedry himself, who complains to Hammond about how little he's being paid. The fact that Nedry can retaliate by bringing the entire park to a screeching standstill with the click of a button certainly speaks to corners cut at the development stage.

Nedry is even further removed from the reality of the dinosaurs-qua-dinosaurs than Hammond is: they are not living creatures but a potential source of money and thus a logistical problem to be solved. In his single face-to-face encounter with a dinosaur — the frilled and venom-spitting dilophosaurus — Nedry's ignorance and disrespect spell his doom. Dilophosaurus is one of the most inaccurately represented dinosaurs in the movie; in real life, she was a seven-meter-long theropod who didn't need a distracting frill or paralyzing spit to subdue her victims. She did it the old-fashioned way, with teeth and claws. In her cinematic redesign, dilophosaurus is small and dainty, even harmless seeming; Nedry treats her like a dog, trying to get her to play fetch before dismissing her as stupid — "no wonder you're extinct" — and promising to run her over with his jeep. The movie's additions to the dilophosaurus make her positively yonic, a vagina dentata come to life, and the one-two punch of flapping open her enormous neck frills before spitting venom into Nedry's eyes is a real heavy-handed reminder to respect nature. As Nedry is consumed, we watch the nifty fake Barbasol can in which he had concealed dinosaur embryos get buried in mud, Nature taking her daughters back until they're ready to return in a bloated sequel.

Compared to Dr. Grant calmly luring a brachiosaurus to eat a leafy branch from his hands, or Dr. Sattler inspecting the nodules on the sick triceratops's tongue, Nedry's impatience, greed, disrespect, and above all *haste* signify the worst version of technocapitalism, one fixated on the possibilities of exploitation and profit with no consideration of moral responsibility or possible consequences. Despite the tidiness of these character foils, though, the movie gives us a third model of academic identity, beyond the digger and the innovator: the public intellectual.

DINOSAUR ECOLOGIES

There's been a meme going around lately that gays all dress like characters from *Jurassic Park*, and as much as I would love to be a Laura Dern gay, in her knotted shirt and khaki shorts and big, practical boots, tromping through the jungle and leaping tree branches to evade velociraptors, I am, alas, a Jeff Goldblum gay, all fun glasses and statement jewelry and a little too much cleavage for an academic setting. But that's appropriate, because I'm also an Ian Malcolm kind of academic; I'm very good at the big picture, at ruining lunch by yelling at men, and at writing cool, sexy books that everyone wants to read, like this one. In part inspired by historian of science James Gleick, Dr. Malcolm is characterized by his interest in the ethical ramifications of fucking with complex systems and his alleged celebrity, which the movie gestures to by dressing him all in black and making him chew gum. His role as a trendy intellectual-for-hire is more poignantly and effectively invoked in *Jurassic World Dominion*, one of the only things the sixth film in the franchise does better than the original; Malcolm has been hired by Biosyn to be its forewarner-in-residence, cautioning the ambitious young tech workers about the consequences of what they're doing, signing their copies of his book, and then watching them return to business as usual, his presence there lending the work a veneer of legitimacy and critical self-reflection.

In *Jurassic Park*, however, his role is more straightforward; he's something of a wise-cracking audience surrogate, repeatedly warning about and thus foreshadowing all the ways in which the park is inevitably going to go wrong. His ability to write populist scholarly work is connected to his ability to speak directly to us, the viewers, while Drs. Grant and Sattler register as a bit odd, too deeply concerned with their scientific discoveries to communicate with regular people (Dr. Grant threatens a child with a claw to prove a point about evolution; Dr. Sattler mutters to herself while elbow-deep in shit). Theirs is the slow and deep work that counters the dangerous speed of discovery and technological development, that is reluctantly reliant upon but ultimately unfaithful to capitalism. And while they aren't the same voice of ethical disapproval that Dr. Malcolm is, their careful approach nonetheless leads to the same conclusions.

We ultimately don't know if Hammond could have successfully bought Grant's and Sattler's endorsements with the promise of ongoing funding; by the end of the film, the disastrous results of human interaction with dinosaurs are so apparent that everyone agrees the park was a very bad idea. What we do know is that Malcolm, with his understanding of the unpredictability of complex systems, is against the whole thing from the start. In a way, his thinking is downright ecological.

And yet, for all our contemporary understanding of eco-systems and their importance, when we picture dinosaurs, we tend to wrench them out of their original surroundings and drop them into new environs: a museum exhibit, an island theme park, downtown New York City. In "What Were Dinosaurs For?" Verlyn Klinkenborg links this tendency to how bad we are at imagining ancient ecosystems, understanding that dinosaurs lived on an Earth that both was and was not this one, and thus that "we as a species are descended not only from the tiny mammals alive at the time, scurrying nocturnally among the dinosaurs, but from their ecosystem as a whole, which shaped both dinosaurs and mammals together." The worlds in which dinosaurs lived — many worlds, over 180 million years — were profoundly alien and yet also our own, in a literal sense: the worlds from which we are descended.

In "Pale/ontology: The Dinosaurian Critique of Philosophy," a whimsical discussion of how dinosaurs challenge Western philosophy, Sam Kriss links the human fascination with these ancient creatures to "the uncomfortable feeling that they might somehow *come back*" alongside what we imagine them doing if or when they return. And what they almost always do, it seems, is start destroying infrastructure, a baffling tendency considering that there's no way a dinosaur would be able to tell the difference between a building and a tree, a jeep and a rock. "Clearly it's not the buildings themselves the dinosaurs object to," writes Kriss, "it's the spatial logic that they represent, the system by which we parcel out the topology of existence into named and comprehensible chunks." For humans, these distinctions matter because they are part of how we constitute ourselves as subjects, the ones who stand at the center of existence and label it, like Adam naming the animals. To dinosaurs, though, we are not subjects; we are dinner.

Jurassic Park draws distinctly postcolonial connections between tourism, scientific discovery, naturalism, zookeeping, and the many other industries that involve human attempts to manage and control, to impose our image on, nature. That's why all the true villains of the franchise are humans — power hungry tech CEOs, greedy lawyers, and, in later movies, straight-up war criminals who train dinosaurs to attack on sight. The dinosaurs themselves are not good or bad. What they are is wild.

REWILDING

Wild does not mean natural, though. The wild is not always the opposite of human interference, claims Helen Macdonald in *H Is for Hawk*: "The wild can be human work." The first time I read Macdonald's memoir of grief and falconry, I couldn't help but make connections to my own experience of parental loss and its reverberations with the idea of wildness. My hippie mother, with her overgrown garden and passion for plant-based medicines, was also an ardent defender of rewilding. Rewilding is the attempt to remove human intervention from ecosystems, to support them once more into self-sustainability. It's a controversial notion in the world of conservation, entangled as it is with contested categories like human versus animal, natural versus artificial, and conservation versus restoration. Is there such thing as an ecosystem devoid of human intervention in the 21st century? What are the ethics of culling invasive species in the name of restoring a previous ecosystem?

In my mother's practice, though, rewilding was about doing less. Her great triumph, during her short life, was convincing the City of Ottawa to stop mowing a patch of grass in Windsor Park, near the Rideau River. I imagine if she tried the same thing today, the main opposition would be the risk of ticks (an escalating danger spurred by, what else, human-caused climate change), but back in the '90s you could walk through a field of waist-high grass without worrying about Lyme disease. And thanks to my mom, I did, in a strip of a field between a road and the park's elevated path, built to protect nearby homes from the river's annual flooding — a field that was wild enough to feed bees and butterflies but not so wild that it endangered human infrastructure. She wasn't naive, my hippie mother. She just liked pollinators.

Like my mother's wild-grass-filled field, the wildness of the dinosaurs in *Jurassic Park* is human work. Together, humans and dinosaurs have "conspired to strangeness," as Macdonald words it. They are man-made, these dinosaurs, as rewilded landscapes inevitably are, and there are things about them we got wrong — the feathers, for example, or the T. rex's sight. They both are and are not animals, are and are not natural. Narratively they stand in for a wildness that is directly opposed to technology, but cinematically they are the products of a technology so advanced that it almost seems like magic.

Their wildness is, of course, part of the appeal: to get up close to wildness itself but in a safe and managed way, in the form of exhibits and guided tours. What Hammond and his team want to do is drag the deep past into the present and, in so doing, pull that wildness, that otherness, into our systems of understanding: the lab and the zoo, the theme park and the museum. There is a violence to this desire that Hammond names "discovery," but Dr. Malcolm recognizes as a form of colonialism. "What's so great about discovery?" he demands. "It's a violent, penetrative act that scars what it explores. What you call discovery, I call the rape of the natural world." Hammond hasn't reintroduced a species killed by human intervention; he isn't actually trying to rewild dinosaurs but to *un*wild them, to make them knowable and manageable. Hammond may turn naturalist in the second movie, but Malcolm is right to be skeptical of the possibility of eliminating human intervention — or dinosaur intervention into human systems, as it turns out.

Hammond's terrible park may evoke circuses and zoos and safaris, but the animal nature of the dinosaurs is not sufficient to explain their deadliness or their chaotic power. The park workers are, after all, professionals who have ostensibly dealt with lions and big snakes and stuff, and yet things go wrong so very quickly. Dr. Grant gives us a hint as to why when he says of the T. rex, "You can't just suppress 65 million years of gut instinct." IMDb lists this line as an error; T. rex only existed as a species for two to three million years and has been *extinct* for 65 million years.

But what if it's not a mistake? What this line suggests is that these cloned dinosaurs, wrenched from their original contexts and violently relocated into the present, bring with them the force of that massive stretch of time. That, behind the bite of the T. rex, the horns of the triceratops, the eye of the velociraptor, is 65 million years of history and an unspeakable divide that separates their world from ours. Their ferocity is the ferocity of deep time: they aren't just dinosaurs, they're chthonic forces, ancient goddesses who have awakened furious and hungry. Hammond's scientists may want to claim parenthood of these creatures, but dinosaurs come from the earth and from the past as well as from the lab. And they don't arrive alone: they bring their wildness with them.

In so doing, they remind us that the Earth has not always been our place. That it might not be our place even now. That for all our desire to impose order on the world, at the end of the day, chaos reigns.

3

"You never had control — that's the illusion!": Chaos, Apocalypse, and Queer Family-Making

There are no mothers in *Jurassic Park*. Ellie wants kids one day; Hammond's daughter, the mother of his grandchildren, is mentioned in passing (she's going through a divorce); all of the dinosaurs we encounter were bred in a lab, motherless; and while Dr. Grant finds empty eggs and tiny dinosaur footprints, whatever queer miracle of creation has taken place happened entirely offscreen. The rest of the franchise is basically obsessed with mothers, but here they are almost conspicuously absent, and the kinships that take their place speak to a queerly expansive understanding of family. As Zena Sharman explains in *The Care We Dream Of*, extending our understanding of family beyond the limits of biology (e.g., birth parents) and the state (e.g., marriage) is vital to queer and trans survival:

"Normative concepts like the nuclear family or 'next of kin' aren't expansive enough to contain the myriad ways queer and trans people relate to each other and create family. LGBTQ+ people have a long tradition of creating family and caring for each other in the face of harm or rejection by our families of origin, government inaction, or outright aggression, and laws and policies that don't recognize our relationships to each other." Queer and chosen family are not about the absence of traditional family figures but rather about a capacious redefinition of what family can mean, and this redefinition is far from superficial. Queer and trans people, writes Sharman, are "practised at fostering relationships grounded in a commitment to our mutual survival."

Having become motherless while still a child, I tend to notice when mothers are absent. This is both a resonance of my own loss and hard-earned experience. When my mom was sick, I would go to the local movie rental shop and bring her home a stack of old releases. West Coast Video was less than ten minutes from our house, a favored destination from when I only frequented the tiny children's section in the back, with four-foot-high shelves and shrunken plastic chairs and entries in their latest coloring contest taped to the walls. It was the kind of neighborhood video shop I miss the most, with a popcorn machine on the front counter filling the store with artificial butter smell and bulk deals on renting older movies. That's where I rented *The Last Unicorn* every week for months on end and where, as a teen, I surreptitiously read the plot summaries on erotic thrillers like *Poison Ivy*, and it's where I once made the terrible choice to rent my mother a copy of *Stepmom*, in which a terminally ill Susan Sarandon learns to embrace her husband's new, much younger wife. As you may imagine, my own terminally ill mother did not take kindly to the message of this movie, and I learned an important lesson about checking for dying-mom content.

Children's media often kills off mothers, frequently before the story has even begun. I read this motherlessness as a trope of maturation: growing up means leaving your mother behind, in favor of mature (heterosexual, reproductive) relationships. Not the case in *Jurassic Park*, where the absence of mothers means everyone else needs to step the fuck up, whether by learning to nurture children (Dr. Grant cradling Lex and Tim in the arms of a tree, promising to stay awake all night) or to reproduce otherwise. In *Lost World* we're introduced to mummy and daddy T. rexes fretting over their baby, so heavily overwritten by heteronormative scripts that they might as well be wearing a little tie and fake eyelashes so we can tell which is which. In *Jurassic Park*, though, things are not quite so orderly.

Patriarchal cultures throughout history (the Mesopotamians, the Ancient Greeks, the early Christians) have associated chaos with femininity and order with masculinity, often via creation myths in which a hero slays a serpent or dragon, a monstrous mommy who must be destroyed or caged in service of the creation of an orderly and differentiated world. In the myth of the Babylonian serpent goddess Tiamat, for example, the warrior-god Marduk defeats her and her army of monsters and dragons, then rips her body apart to create an ordered world: the heavens and the earth, the rivers and the mountains. If you were raised on second-wave feminism like me, you've probably already heard theories that tales of dragon-slaying knights reinvoke these myths, showing heroic men repeatedly, violently ripping order from the undifferentiated chaos of a monstrous woman's body. But as feminist readers we must ask: who gets to define chaos and order? Who is served by the violent imposition of this binary? What if the chaos that has been repeatedly associated with women is not chaos at all, but another way of being with its own logics, logics that patriarchal worldviews seek to reject?

As a girl, I was surrounded by stories about what it meant to be good and how that goodness would be rewarded. Always lurking at the edge of those stories was the promise of an orderly life: maturation from girl into woman, then marriage, then children. And sure, on the surface *Jurassic Park* tells a similar story: Grant goes from being a person who doesn't want kids to a person who does. Hammond goes from a venture capitalist who thinks cloning dinosaurs is a great idea to an appropriately doting grandfather who cares more for the safety of his grand-children than the success of his park. Cue the restoration of orderly domestic happiness, a classic Spielbergian ending. But underneath that neat conclusion, other possibilities lurk.

SLOW APOCALYPSE

Early in the movie, as Drs. Grant, Sattler, and Malcolm consider the strangeness of the park's premise, an iconic exchange occurs:

Malcolm: God creates dinosaurs. God destroys dinosaurs. God creates man. Man destroys God. Man creates dinosaurs.

Sattler: Dinosaurs *eat* man. Woman inherits the Earth.

Sattler's intervention here is a reminder of how an order-based vision of the world has no place for women, because women embody the chaos that must be tamed for order to exist. Sattler reverses the patriarchal creation myth; rather than men destroying feminized monsters to remake the world, men's obsession with control leads to their own destruction and women take over. It is no coincidence that woman inherits the Earth *after* the dinosaurs have eaten the men, a matriarchal society emerging in the wake of a dinosaur-led apocalypse.

What is an apocalypse, after all, but the retreat of order into chaos, the undoing of the differentiation of so many creation myths. Etymologically and in its earliest usages, apocalypse means "uncovering" or "revelation," coming from the Greek word for pulling the lid off something. I think immediately of Pandora's box, the insatiably curious girl accidentally unleashing a horde of curses, like monstrous serpents and dragons, upon the world. In the New Testament, the raw destruction of John's apocalyptic imaginings culminates in a new revelation, a new heaven and earth. An apocalypse is both an ending and a beginning, something that might be awful but that still carries the possibility of the new within. The return of chaos, and with it, the potential for re-creation.

My mother's death was a slow apocalypse. I was eight when she was first diagnosed with breast cancer and thirteen when that diagnosis became terminal. She told me she was dying at the end of the summer between eighth and ninth grade; in retrospect, I'm pretty sure I was the last to know, the baby of the family, always a little more sheltered from the cruelties of the world. We were sitting together when she told me, just the two of us snuggled side by side in the enormous plaid armchair that we'd also taken our last family portrait in, one of the final documents of our family before it was broken forever. I was starting high school in just a few weeks and would enter that new environment with a new identity: the girl whose mother was dying.

If you've never lost a loved one to a terminal disease, you might not know all that lies inside that phrase, "was dying." We think of death sometimes as a before and after, as another binary: you're alive or you're not. But for two and a half years, she died. The cancer spread through her body, into her bones and lungs, her pancreas and kidneys and brain. It ate holes in her rib cage and filled her lungs with fluid so that she couldn't breathe without an oxygen machine; we set it up in the basement and drilled a hole in the floor of her room to thread the tube up to her bed. She died in a room we built for that express purpose, using an advance on her life insurance. We lived inside the slow fact of her death, an apocalypse that culminated when I was 16 and she chose to die by suicide, her body ravaged by tumors, her remarkable reserves of patience and fortitude finally exhausted. And it felt, in a totally non-metaphorical way, like the end of the world. The moment I found out she was dead, I thought, "Then I'm going to die too." I couldn't conceive of an after to her, even while I'd been obsessively imagining it for half my life.

While there was some comfort to be had in stories of happy families in the wake of her death, of mothers who stayed alive and fathers who stuck around, of brothers who looked out for you instead of punching holes in the wall, I found myself turning increasingly to stories of apocalypse. I immersed myself in epic fantasy novels where the world had to be torn apart before it could be remade into something else, in disaster movies where I got to cathartically watch cosmopolitan landmarks swallowed by lava or exploded by aliens, the flagrant depictions of global destruction mirroring how I felt inside. I feel a similar hunger for apocalypses now, living through a period of history that feels awfully, familiarly chaotic: global pandemics, escalating climate-change-fueled natural disasters, nuclear powers waging wars of expansion while fascism spreads. Surely there is no after to this time that looks anything like the before; and so I turn to stories that imagine what's next, that show people living through the worst possible thing and coming out the other side, changed but still somewhat intact, still doing their best to care for one another in a world turned upside down.

I'm not alone in this hunger; apocalyptic narratives have been zeitgeisty for almost a decade now, in part because humanity is collectively facing down the consequences of centuries of colonialism, capitalism, and white supremacy. But there has also been a surge in apocalyptic and post-apocalyptic storytelling by Black and Indigenous artists, stories that use the post-apocalyptic not as a vision of what might come but as a way of representing the world that Black and Indigenous people are already living in. As Sisseton Wahpeton Oyate scholar Kim TallBear states in a 2022 talk entitled "A Sharpening of the Already Present: Apocalypse and Radical Hope," Indigenous Peoples have already lived through an apocalypse:

> Dakota people's apocalyptic grieving has a long timeline; we are at a different stage of grief. The genocide over hundreds of years of Indigenous peoples in the Americas and the co-decimation of nonhuman relatives and their societies brings us and you to here. It is *this* world built out of *our* apocalypse that is now at risk. Dakota people grieve what this world still celebrates in its doctrines, anthems, explosions, and glorious accounts.

That apocalypse was the colonization of the Americas and the ensuing slow death, via disease and state-sanctioned murder and displacement and cultural genocide, of roughly 90% of the pre-contact population. That apocalypse was the transatlantic slave trade, in which 12 million Africans were kidnapped and forcibly relocated, millions of whom died on the Middle Passage, millions more of whom died under the violence of slavery itself. When white people declare that the current historical moment feels like the end of the world, we risk erasing the ends of worlds that have come before, in which we are unavoidably entangled and complicit, and ignoring how our contemporary crises also emerged from the long apocalypse of colonization and slavery, how we have wrought these horrors ourselves by treating the world as something we can endlessly plunder without consequence.

Not all apocalypses are human-made — but some undeniably are. And ironically, many of these human-made apocalypses emerge from the oppressive systems of order imposed on the world, supposedly to hold it back from the brink of chaos. Maybe it isn't the chaos we need to fear; it's the violence of what we do to pretend we have everything under control. The prospect of change is terrifying, but the prospect of continuing as we are now is so much worse.

TAKING CARE

The scientists in *Jurassic Park* have bred an apocalypse: by bringing dinosaurs back into the world, they have done something profoundly transformative and completely irreversible. They have unleashed onto humanity a revelation of tooth and scale, opened a Pandora's box chockablock full of things that want to eat them, and that lid is not going back on. Once you unleash chaos into the world, you cannot leash it again — that's what all the subsequent movies are about — but this first one ends so ambiguously, not with T. rex roaring triumphantly as a banner reading "When Dinosaurs Ruled the Earth" flutters down around her, telling us that this past has been irrevocably collapsed into our present, but with birds, a flock of brown pelicans to be precise, flying low over the surface of the ocean.

Those birds tell us: dinosaurs aren't *back*, they've been here the whole time. They say: the world has not suddenly *become* wild and dangerous, it has always been so, and any fantasies of control were just fantasies. The dinosaurs have changed something, yes, but they've also revealed something that has always been true, something that, deep in our DNA, we've suspected all along. Dinosaurs are the bones of the ancient Earth, reminding us that she's been ancient and full of bones this whole time, while we've been slithering around on her surface pretending to be in charge, gleefully extracting resources from her and pretending we'll never have to reap the consequences.

Those consequences sure are reaped in *Jurassic Park*. But while hubris is one of the top crimes in the movie (punishable by death-by-dinosaur), it's overshadowed by the most serious transgression: failure to care for children. Consider the final scene of the movie, with Lex and Tim sleeping in Dr. Grant's arms while Dr. Sattler looks on, smiling. Sure, there's one reading where Sattler has successfully inducted Grant into the cult of heterosexual reproduction. But they aren't Lex and Tim's parents, and they also won't go on to have children together. From the beginning of the movie, Sattler has been trying to convince Grant to simply . . . give kids a chance. To consider them as "small versions of adults," as she puts it, rather than the incomprehensible alien creatures he seems to view them as, and to voluntarily be in their company because it will be "good for him."

And it *is* good for him, as it is good for the children; they keep each other alive and care for each other. When a mud-soaked Lex, freshly rescued from the T. rex, whimpers that Gennaro (the weaselly lawyer, in case you forgot) left them, Grant looks her in the eye and vows, "But that's not what I'm going to do." In Sattler's satisfied smile, I see the triumph of the matriarch, a glimmer of women inheriting the Earth after dinosaurs have eaten *most* of the men, and *all* of the men who reneged on their duties of care.

And the dinosaurs do, in *Jurassic Park*, eat only men. There are two directly opposing ways to interpret this hunger for male flesh in particular. The first is to point out that women and children almost never die in American action movies. That's because action movies mirror the Western logics of war — men can go off to die in service of the greater good, but white women and children must be protected at all costs to ensure the reproductive futurity of the nation. If we do see women and children die, they're probably unnamed and racialized background characters. In *Jurassic Park*, that war movie logic applies: only men die for humanity, as is their duty.

The reading I prefer, however, is to see the dinosaurs as participating in some kind of sapphic fantasy, complete with a misandrist death drive, like the amazons on Themyscira killing any man who dares pollute their sacred shores. According to that logic, only the men who fall in line get to make it out alive:

Grant, who has kept the children safe; Malcolm, who sacrificed himself to lead the T. rex away from the children; and their grandfather, who fucked up royally but whose death would probably traumatize them quite deeply. In this post-apocalyptic and dinosaur-filled world, the gendered logics of care have no place; in a world turned upside down, you either step up or get eaten.

Let me pause for a beat here and talk about my concern with childcare. *But Hannah*, you might be saying, *aren't you a childless spinster? How can you call this a feminist movie if it's about looking after children? Isn't it retrograde to associate feminism with childcare?* It's true, I am a spinster, and also a gay auntie, and most importantly I am committed to enacting my feminist politics as an orientation toward collective rather than individual liberation, which means looking beyond my personal concerns with how my life is treated as less-than because I haven't put my uterus to use. That means, rather than focusing solely on access to abortion and the right to not have children, I am concerned with reproductive justice. This framework was created by Women of African Descent for Reproductive Justice and popularized by the SisterSong Women of Color Reproductive Justice Collective in the 1990s to critique how the predominantly white women's rights movement focused on safe and legal abortion at the expense of issues such as forced sterilization, child apprehension by the state, and maternal mortality rates, all of which disproportionately impact Black and Indigenous communities.

What is happening to the dinosaurs in *Jurassic Park* is eerily parallel to the way that Black and Indigenous people, disabled and Mad people, migrants, and other precaritized communities have been treated in white supremacist states: they have been incarcerated, forcibly sterilized, their offspring kidnapped into institutions by white men who claim to be acting from a place of benevolence. Film scholars Laura Briggs and Jodi I. Kelber-Kaye read the uncontrolled reproduction of the dinosaurs as a symbol of anxiety about uncontrolled "Third World" reproduction, the dinosaurs standing in for racialized women whose fertility, if not managed by Western scientists, risks overrunning and overpopulating the world. The flip side of this genocidal desire to control the reproduction of racialized people is the desire to force white women to fulfill the promise of reproductive futurity. As Interrupting Criminalization's 2022 brief *We Must Fight in Solidarity with Trans Youth* explains, anti-trans legislation and the stripping away of abortion rights are both rooted in the white supremacist "great replacement" theory, which holds that people of color are "replacing" white people and thus that white people with uteruses must be made to produce more white babies for a white nation, whether we want to or not.

Like so many harmful ideologies, this belief that it is the primary social function of white women to reproduce the white race is deeply embedded in our everyday lives. I know what it is like, viscerally, to be told that my life matters less because I have neither partnered nor reproduced, to have my experiences of the world and my capacity for care dismissed because I'm "not a mom" and "wouldn't understand." I see how differently I'm treated on the street, by strangers, if I'm taking a friend's kid for a walk, and then the suspicious turn when they find out it's not my child. Even my own friends have half joked that I'm planning on stealing their children, a crone luring unsuspecting infants into her gingerbread house.

The specter of the childless woman is terrifying. What are we getting up to with all that free time? What schemes might we be hatching in our well-rested brains; what monsters are our empty wombs gestating? But none of this translates into mothers being privileged. That's the trap of patriarchy, after all: you're damned if you do, damned if you don't. Mothers in our society are surveilled, policed, and judged, in ways that are amplified by class, race, disability, and other intersections of oppression; the childless crone may be a monstrous figure, but so are mothers. Their capacity for reproduction is a trait that men both need and despise, hence the way Western literature is littered with monstrous mommies who give birth to other monsters or who pervert the proper cycle of motherhood by consuming their own children.

My own family's history is littered with motherlessness. My mother's mother, Joan, was a war bride, married during the Second World War miles from her family. In the letters her bridesmaids sent her mother — letters we have because Joan saved them her entire life, in a small file of precious things — they describe how hard it was for Joan to be married without her mother there, reassuring Mrs. Hodsdon that they played the role of mother in her stead, kissing Joan as she woke. When Joan sailed across the Atlantic with tens of thousands of other war brides to join a husband she hadn't seen in years, her mother began writing her immediately, mourning Joan's abrupt departure, that they hadn't had enough time to say goodbye properly and were now separated by a vast ocean and by Joan's new role as wife and mother. My aunt found these letters only after her mother had died, a window onto a woman she had barely known holding onto a grief she had never shared. There are a lot of ways to lose your mother, and not all of them involve death.

Jurassic Park is not just a survival movie — it is a feminist apocalypse that asserts matriarchal, care-based values in the face of a crisis of motherlessness. It's a story that uses the narrative function of chaos to assert how many forms of care are possible beyond patriarchal binaries and that explicitly values that care. This is why I loved the movie on first viewing, and why I've returned to it so many times throughout my life: it became part of my own tool kit for surviving apocalypse.

A TOOL KIT FOR THE APOCALYPSE

I never properly finished eighth grade: my mother went to the principal and convinced them that I could finish with self-directed study at home. There were lots of academic justifications (I was moving from an enriched program to a general program, so I was ahead academically; I had already been accepted into the arts high school I would start attending the following year), but the reality was that I was socially miserable, a bullied outcast who more often than not ended up in physical altercations with the boys who loathed me, a loud, smart, fat girl, tall and strong and not particularly concerned with their opinions of me. And beneath that justification, another, deeper one, which I've only started to understand recently. She knew, by then, that she was dying and had begun to look for ways that we could spend more time together.

So for the second half of eighth grade, my mother oversaw my education, teaching me how to follow my own curiosity, how to ask questions and then hunt down the answers. I developed three deep fascinations during that time: goth fashion, the Paris salons of the 1930s, and plate tectonics. That goth phase carried me into high school; I showed up for eighth-grade graduation in torn fishnets, a spiked dog collar, and Doc Martens, every bit the overly self-conscious art student I was about to become. I fell in love with Paris via Gertrude Stein's *The Autobiography of Alice B. Toklas*, a book that offered me a glimpse of a lineage of queer artists and weirdos who didn't fit in and so made their own worlds, in defiance of the status quo. But my interest in plate tectonics wasn't really new — it was a revival of my enduring fascination with the prehistoric world and, of course, dinosaurs.

I hadn't had the chance to study them formally since second grade, when I remember making a plasticine sculpture of a duck-billed dinosaur, which I also remember being very good and realistic. (It's lost to time now, so you'll have to take my word.) If Paris of the 1930s made the world feel like it might have a place for me, Pangaea made the world seem unutterably strange, which was equally comforting in its way. All those happy people who seemed to fit in so effortlessly, to find their place without pain or confusion, the pretty girls and athletic boys, they simply didn't understand that the Earth was ancient and unspeakably strange, that the seemingly stable landscape had been torn from the white hot guts of our planet by the slow grinding migration of continents over millions of years, that the moment we were living in was not the end of history but rather a blip in a story too vast for any of us to comprehend, so vast, in fact, that a single person's prettiness or athleticism was totally insignificant.

When my mother cuddled up with me in that plaid arm-chair that was as wide as it was tall and told me that her cancer diagnosis had become terminal, I had already gathered some of the intellectual and artistic tools that would help me navigate her death: black lipstick, the art of people who had just lived through the First World War, and a deeper sense of the Earth's history as a series of apocalypses big and small, from extinction events to continents smashing into each other and creating mountain ranges. Each of these apocalypses had been both terrifying and world-making. I couldn't imagine living after my mother died, but people did, it turned out; they lived through all kinds of things, things that changed them forever. This was the beauty and the horror at the heart of chaos. The ordered world I'd been promised if I was good enough turned out to be a lie. That realization was horrifying, but it also set me free in a way; if being a good girl couldn't protect me from chaos, then maybe being good wasn't the point.

When Dr. Sattler claims that women will inherit the Earth, she is not just staking a claim on the matriarchal outcomes of the movie; she is also denying the teleological history that Dr. Malcolm traces with his god/dinosaur/man aphorism. Teleology is the idea that history is inevitably progressing toward some end point or goal. Nature writer Verlyn Klinkenborg calls teleology "the moralizing of chronology" and points to how insidiously it slips into our understanding of history and our place in it: "Because we come after, it's easy to suppose we must be the purpose of what came before." That logical fallacy is at work in a lot of popular understandings of evolution, which is treated as a straight line from non-ideal to ideal forms, rather than what it actually is: a series of random and microscopic changes, some of which end up helping a species to survive.

Despite being a theorist of chaos, Dr. Malcolm has a tendency to get a little teleological when he talks about Nature. In his desire to convince a bunch of truly terrible and hubris-filled men to pause and think about what they're doing, he overattributes to Nature a level of intentionality and design at odds with the chaos he believes in. "Dinosaurs had their chance," he tells Hammond, "and Nature selected them for extinction." That's not quite right, though, is it? The whole point of natural selection is that no one is doing the selecting; the world changes through a series of unpredictable and chaotic events, and the very traits that might have once made you a dominant species are now no longer suited to the world as it exists. The dinosaurs didn't die out because someone had a plan, or made a choice, or intended anything at all; it didn't happen for a reason. It just happened.

To quote Klinkenborg again, "the obvious, quotidian logic of chronology is basically too much for the human mind: we're constantly confusing sequence, causation, and purpose." Chronology lacks morality: this thing happened, and then this other thing happened. We reach for narrative to make sense of it, and because we're humans, the narratives we reach for are often deeply ideological, reinforcing our own natural dominance or our importance in the grand scheme of things, insisting that events happen *for* us rather than *to* us. Part of the reason for this navel-gazing tendency is how bad we are — humans, I mean — at understanding deep time and our own insignificance. As Klinkenborg puts it, "we can't feel it in our bones." Geologists tend to reach for metaphors and analogies to explain it, like writer John McPhee's yard measurement: "Consider the Earth's history as the old measure of the English yard, the distance from the king's nose to the tip of his out-stretched hand. One stroke of a nail file on his middle finger erases human history."

When we think too much about deep time, it can have a vertiginous effect, the disorientation of zooming out so far that we lose perspective altogether, like trying to find an unfamiliar intersection in a strange country on Google Maps. We can think about time, it seems, or we can think about ourselves, but we're bad at thinking about both simultaneously.

But for a long time now, I've found the vertigo of deep time comforting. It's one of the surefire ways I can calm my poor, feverish, anxiety-ridden brain when it gets overwhelmed: by thinking about the size of space or the age of the Earth. That desire to feel existentially small stems, I think, from my mother's death. The terrifying reality of a world without her made so much more sense once I remembered that there was a world without all of us in it, that, in fact, we are a fingernail shaving on the long arm of history, that the Earth itself is a baby within an unbearably old universe, that existence predates us significantly and will continue long after us and in the blink of an eye we'll all be less than a memory. It soothes me to think that things just happen, for no particular reason. That sometimes people get cancer and die, and it isn't because Nature selected them for extinction, or because someone else needed to learn an important lesson about impermanence; it's just chaos. It was so much easier to let her go, to weather the personal apocalypse of her death, when I realized that the world I had been holding on to, one in which mothers were ever-present and stable sources of love, was only ever an illusion.

As Dr. Sattler puts it, we never had control. That's the illusion.

FEELING YOUR WAY THROUGH

Dr. Malcolm understands lack of control theoretically — he is, after all, a chaotician, an expert in chaos theory. Chaos theory is a subfield of mathematics perhaps best known via the concept of the butterfly effect: the idea that some systems are so complex as to be functionally random, such that a tiny shift in initial conditions (the flapping of a butterfly's wing in Brazil) can impact large-scale phenomena (a tornado in Texas) unpredictably. Despite its name, chaos theory is not truly about the absence of order; it's about complexity and sensitivity. For all his theoretical understanding of the chaos that inevitably ensues at Jurassic Park, Malcolm isn't as good at leaning into that chaos, which is, at least thematically speaking, why he gets pretty badly chomped by that T. rex early on and has to spend the rest of the movie reclining with his shirt open.

This is another real Hannah move, by the way. I'm good at understanding things theoretically and yelling about them, but it's a new skill for me to understand things viscerally, or somatically, in my body. That's a trauma response (don't worry about it), but I do see it playing out onscreen as our characters all respond to the horrors of the dinosaurs running loose, of Hammond's grandchildren and Dr. Grant being lost somewhere in the park, of Gennaro and then Nedry and then Arnold and then Muldoon being eaten, of the velociraptors quickly escalating from testing fences to turning doorknobs to, we can only assume, operating heavy machinery. And while I learned many of the lessons of *Jurassic Park* early — lessons about the potential beauty of monstrosity, and the importance of staying very, very still — it took me a much longer time to listen to Ellie Sattler when she tells Hammond that the chaos of the park isn't something he can solve with better systems and more control: "You can't think your way through this, John. You have to feel it."

There's one reading of this line that says *oh cool we made the only lady talk about feelings*, and that reading absolutely resonates with me because I am a lady, sort of, and I've certainly been made responsible for a lot of men's feelings. Doing the emotional labor of processing everyone's emotions for them is exhausting work, and in my experience, it's work that you have to reject, repeatedly and deliberately, if you are someone who is read as a woman. And rejecting that labor is also dangerous, just like any refusal to be the way men want you to be is dangerous. But in this moment, Sattler isn't comforting Hammond; she's showing him the violence his supposedly ordered and rational world has visited upon his own loved ones and demanding that he stop pretending to have control. Her insistence on feeling is an ethical intervention into the patriarchal world of progress for progress's sake, a specifically feminist intervention that asserts the wisdom of the body and of the emotions. What Sattler is saying is "listen to the part of your body that is terrified right now, and learn the lesson of that fear." Staying alive by listening to fear is, after all, a skill many women learn very early in our lives.

The problem comes when, like Lex, you're kind of afraid of everything. Poor Lex, awkward teen hacker, a bit of a wet blanket, for all that her fear of dinosaurs makes *extremely good sense*. Grant isn't a dick about it, either, helping her to better understand the dinosaurs and navigate their threat level but never underplaying the severity of the situation, or of her trauma. In fact, a healthy dose of fear ultimately keeps all the survivors alive, as if the dinosaurs are hungry for overconfidence. But I identify with Lex in those moments when she's reduced to a gibbering mess, Jell-O shaking on her spoon. There is a part of me that is also comprised of raw fear. I don't know where that part came from; it predates my mother's illness, my first encounters with scary books or movies. It's like I was born afraid: of the dark, of heights, of deep water, of falling, of hurting myself, of strangers, of unfamiliar places, of trying new things.

And so when people have told me to listen to my fear, my response has often been that I can't, otherwise I'd never do anything. Swallowing my fear has allowed me to build the life I have, to travel and meet new people, to pursue a competitive and difficult career, to move over 4,000 kilometers from my family, to speak back to powerful authority figures and stand up for what I believe in. Swallowing my fear is essential to my feminism; it lets me be ferocious and angry in the face of disapproval and threats of violence. It lets me say the awkward thing, the scary thing, even the dangerous thing. And along the way, I've learned to swallow a whole bevy of other feelings: I swallowed my grief to move on after my mother's death; I swallowed my loneliness to move alone, time and time again, for the sake of an uncertain career. I have swallowed and swallowed until my belly was swollen with unspoken feelings. Like Hammond, I insisted that total control was possible if you just considered and then prepared for every possible variable.

But like Hammond, my pain and grief and trauma and fear were not things I could think my way through; they were, in fact, things I had to feel. Hammond represents a fundamentally broken understanding of the world, one in which men with money and ambition have the right to impose their will on the world, regardless of the consequences. When Sattler tells him to feel his way through, she's advocating against a progress-oriented technocratic viewpoint and for an ethics of care. So many systems of determining right and wrong, of trying to work through how to treat others well and how to organize society in a way that will minimize harm, are based in an understanding of human beings as primarily autonomous individuals. But an ethics of care tells us that we are all interconnected, part of a series of complex systems of interdependence and mutual reliance, and that these systems, for all their complexity, also make us much stronger. Systems thinking is care thinking, and vice versa; if I know that what I do will have an impact on you as well, then I have a responsibility to think through those larger consequences. You might, for example, contribute to the care of children in your community even though you have not chosen to have children yourself. An ethics of care thus presents us with the possibility of living otherwise, of expanding our sense of kin and community.

Jurassic Park is a study in the violence of a worldview that believes control is desirable or even possible. Hammond creates the park because he's obsessed with the idea of engineering the ultimate spectacle, something that people have never seen before, and he believes that "creation is an act of sheer will." He and his scientists seem to believe that progress for progress's sake is an inherently good thing. In this sense, it's a sort of *Frankenstein* story, a critique of the patriarchal drive toward discovery and progress without any sense of responsibility to that which you create. If "woman inherits the Earth," as Sattler puts it, it isn't out of any essentialist biological imperative. It's because the dinosaurs, like those serpent goddesses of myth, are antithetical to these patriarchal ideals of rationality and control. Released into a world where they do not belong, they have no recourse but to destroy it. And as with all apocalypses, we cannot truly know what comes next. We just have to take care of each other as best we can.

ABANDON HOPE, ABANDON FEAR

When my mother was dying, she started going to a day hospice, a service meant to provide respite and care for terminally ill people still living at home. They had foot reflexology and gentle harp music, and best of all people who weren't afraid of talking about death. Even there, though, my mother was a bit much for some of the other patients. She had a homemade T-shirt that read "abandon hope, abandon fear," a Buddhist teaching that had become vital to her as she lived inside the fact of her years-long death. Breast cancer discourse is wrapped in a cloying coating of toxic positivity, with "look good, feel better" campaigns advocating for people to put on a happy face and those who manage to not die celebrated as "survivors" who "won their fight" (implying, I suppose, that the dead are losers). Into this environment stomped Teresa Joan Penner, audaciously braless and one-breasted, toting her abandonment of hope, her willingness to look her own end in the eye — her embrace, you might say, of chaos.

What can we learn from living through an apocalypse? That patriarchal, capitalist, and white supremacist systems of control are illusions, wrenching a semblance of order from violent subjugation and naming anything outside that order "chaos"? That chaos itself is never truly chaotic but profoundly complex, a complexity that defies control and instead demands other responses rooted in kinship and care? This is one version of what it looks like when dinosaurs eat men so that women and non-binary people and queers and weirdos inherit the Earth: in the absence of fences, we have no choice but to hold each other close.

The chaos that ensues from Hammond's lab-engineered apocalypse is only chaotic in the sense that it rips apart the systems of order imposed by a patriarchal worldview, flipping jeeps and shattering educational displays and forcing men to get over their toxic masculinity real quick. "We can discuss sexism in survival situations when I get back," Dr. Sattler snaps at Hammond as he tries to insist that he should be taking greater physical risks because he's a man. The patriarchal gender binary falls apart, and what remains is everyone doing what needs to be done — including the dinosaurs themselves, who are, after all, only doing what they must to survive. The dinosaurs of *Jurassic Park* have been wrenched out of their time, out of the complex ecosystems in which they evolved and thrived. The wrongness of that is only clear if you acknowledge that the world is a complex system of interdependence, and that within that system, you have much less control than you might have imagined.

Conclusion

Backwards and in Beige Heels

In one of the last shots of *Jurassic Park*, we see a flock of pelicans flying low over the water, a reminder of the theory that has been floated throughout the movie: that dinosaurs evolved into birds. Importantly, though, it's only a theory, pointing to the unknowability of the deep geological past, as well as the profound slowness of processes like evolution. Unknowability triumphs over technological hubris; chaos wins over order; slowness trumps speed; and the monstrous women inherit Isla Nublar — at least, until *Jurassic World* comes along.

Sometimes the easiest way to notice something is through its absence. I don't think my understanding of *Jurassic Park* as a film rife with subversive feminist potential really came together until after I had seen 2015's *Jurassic World*, a contemporary blockbuster that reverses the logics of the original film at every stage. Some of those reversals are obvious: rather than Dr. Sattler tromping through the jungle in huge boots, we now have Bryce Dallas Howard's Claire Dearing in a white suit and beige heels, her impeccable bob becoming increasingly curly throughout the film as a visual symbol of her finally loosening up. In the place of Dr. Grant's non-violent navigation of the dinosaurs' terrain and tender care for Hammond's grandchildren, we have bland action star Chris Pratt as Owen Grady, a navy veteran riding a motorcycle through the jungle and taming velociraptors like a paleontological Cesar Millan.

But most insidious, for me, is how *Jurassic World* reimagines our monstrous woman dinosaurs. The velociraptors have become a stand-in for "natural" femininity, one that can be both understood and tamed, in contrast to the new dinosaurs the park has begun to engineer. It's been 22 years since the events of *Jurassic Park*, and absolutely no one has learned anything. Isla Nublar is now home to a hugely successful and popular theme park, overseen by Claire, the park's operations manager, a #girlboss who needs to learn a few things about the natural order from her hunky dinosaur-whisperer ex. Specifically, Claire needs to learn that it was a bad idea to breed a murder dinosaur, the *Indominus rex*, a genetic hybrid whose unnaturalness and literal whiteness link her pretty clearly to Claire as an equally unnatural woman, pristinely and impractically dressed in white and conspicuously unconcerned with the well-being of her visiting nephews. Owen, on the other hand, is all about the natural order of things, whether it's inserting himself into the "pack order" of the velociraptors, killing the *Indominus rex*, or awakening Claire's maternal instincts.

I see myself in the velociraptors in *Jurassic Park*. I identify with their intelligence, their monstrosity, and their queerness. So I take it as a personal affront that, in *Jurassic World*, Owen has turned them into a dog pack. There's a particularly shudder-inducing scene when Claire's nephews, Zach and Gray, first see the raptors. Owen introduces his favorite raptor, Blue, as the pack's beta, which prompts Gray to ask who the alpha is. "You're looking at him, kid," Owen replies with a kind of macho smirk that sends bad shivers down my spine every time I see it.

Did you know that wolf packs in the wild don't actually *have* alphas? That's because they're not hierarchically organized systems, they're families; the so-called dominant wolves are usually just the parents. This confusion arose because early wolf behaviorists studied wolves in captivity, where multiple adult wolves were unnaturally forced together and fought to establish a pecking order. This is what we see in *Jurassic World*: captive animals forced into a battle of dominance that transforms family systems into hierarchies of power, with Owen at the top. And yet the movie is desperate to establish this arrangement as somehow more natural than the other fucked-up stuff going on in the park, like the breeding of the *Indominus rex*. Owen's raptor pack works because he's a "naturally" dominant man who is particularly well suited to controlling semi-feral women. He holds out his hand and, inexplicably, they don't bite it off. (They *do* bite off Vincent D'Onofrio's hand, which I appreciate, but it's too little too late.)

If *Jurassic Park* is about the folly of imagining that nature is controllable, that women are biddable, or that colonialism can be enacted without a terrible cost, then *Jurassic World* is about reinstalling an image of modernity that is perfectly controllable, if only the right white men are in charge. And this is a world in which monstrous women like me have no place.

With the clarity of hindsight, I can see how much of my fondness for Dr. Grant and his care for Lex and Tim stemmed from my own childhood desire to be cared for. As an adult, I know that life is chaos, unpredictable and terrifying, and I know that any attempt to exert control over that chaos backfires rather splendidly. But I also know that one of our responsibilities as adults who love and care for children is to create spaces of respite and security, to cradle them in our arms in the midst of a rampaging dinosaur apocalypse. We cannot remake the world into something controllable; we cannot promise a happy ending. But we can build robust networks of kinship and queer family — in fact, I suspect increasingly that that's *all* we can do. Even wilder, we don't have to make these networks only to care for children; we can also take care of each other, and ourselves.

I have spent much of my life terrified of being left behind. An anxious child, I was afraid of being alone, of not being able to keep up or fit in. As the child of a dying mother, I was terrified of what would become of me once she died; as a motherless child, I lived inside the terror of being cut loose into a world without safety or structure. As a queer, fat, sexually confused youth, I dreaded my own future, knowing that none of the available scripts for a happy life had space for me but unable to imagine anything else. Once I realized I was asexual, that fear of the future intensified: I watched my friends marry and have kids and I swallowed whole the cultural narrative that parents didn't have time for friendships, that I would inevitably be left behind as everyone around me matured into a version of adulthood that I could not make myself want. At the root of these fears is the banal and yet extraordinarily complex problem of not being able to find myself in the stories I loved.

What kinds of happy endings are available for monstrous women? In *Jurassic World*, Blue and the T. rex earn their survival by saving the humans, while *Indominus rex* needs to die, having proven that, even without any humans around, she'll just straight-up murder other dinosaurs for fun. But *Jurassic Park* offers us no such tidy ending: we leave T. rex and the velociraptors in battle, wildness pitted against wildness, the humans removing themselves out of a deep recognition that the island is no longer their place. The chaos of the dinosaurs is not contained or managed but set loose in a world that was never that orderly to begin with, not really, not when we see the ease with which Hammond's empire can crumble. And whatever is next for the dinosaurs and the wildness they have brought with them, we are not privy to it. As the gaze of the camera slides away, from dinosaur to pelican, we ultimately lose sight of those wonders we have been hungrily looking at throughout the movie; the spectacle ends, and we can't know what comes next.

Jurassic Park is the only entry in the franchise to end that way. All the others let the camera, and by extension our gaze, linger on the dinosaurs, reminding us that, no matter how effectively they might have destroyed a theme park or a mansion or an office building, we have maintained control of them by never letting them out of our sight. But in *Jurassic Park*, the attempt to capture and contain the dinosaurs, to render them subject to our endless hunger for spectacle, has failed. We don't know what's been left behind, what the dinosaurs are going to get up to without human intervention. We can't know exactly what it will look like when life finds a way. What we do know is that these angry, monstrous, ravenous women are free, in the way so many of us — queers and feminists, trans and gender-nonconforming folks, Indigenous people and Black people and people of color — long to be. The colonizer has fled, and the dinosaurs are left to make their own way: to thrive, or die, or evolve into birds.

This freedom isn't without its traumas. It's not a utopian vision but an apocalyptic one, a freedom wrenched from the oppressor with tooth and claw. But it's in *that* world, lost to the men who tried to control it, lost to the systems that technocapitalism has attempted to impose, lost even to the benign fascination of scientists like Grant and Sattler — it's in that world that I can imagine a future for a monstrous woman like me, hungry, furious, loud, gay, and prepared to bite your fucking hand off if you call me a girl.

Acknowledgments

Thanks first and foremost to my editor, Jen Sookfong Lee, whose work I've admired for years, long before we met IRL. Thank you for believing in this wacky, angry little book right from the beginning, and for ushering it through the publishing process with such care, like a freshly hatched baby velociraptor.

The kernel of this book was an episode of my podcast *Secret Feminist Agenda*; thanks to everyone who listened to that episode and responded to it with enthusiasm. Once I realized that I wasn't the only queer obsessed with dinosaurs, it was only a matter of time before I turned dinosaurs into my whole personality.

I wrote this book during sabbatical from my job at the publishing program at SFU, an unbelievable privilege that would have been impossible with the support of my tremendous colleagues: Juan Pablo Alperin, Leanne Johnson, John Maxwell, Suzanne Norman, Mauve Pagé, Jo-Anne Ray, and Scott Steedman.

My ability to think about pop culture both critically and joyfully is honed on a regular basis by my collaboration with the Witch, Please Productions "girlies": Gaby Iori, Marcelle Kosman, Zoe Mix, and Hannah Rehak aka Coach. Working with you reminds me of all the things I love most about writing and talking and thinking in community; you make me believe the work matters *and* the work can be fun.

I am lucky enough to be part of a community of artists and writers and organizers and queers and weirdos, people who believe that stories matter and art can change the world, and who live those beliefs in real and material ways. My eternal love and gratitude to Hilary Atleo, Martin Austwick, Dina Del Bucchia, Jessica Delisle, Don English, Cynara Geissler, Brenna Clarke Gray, Lucia Lorenzi, Clare Mulcahy, Aimee Ouellette, Zena Sharman, Bart Vautour, Meghan Waitt, Andrea Warner, Marshall Watson, Erin Wunker, and Helen Zaltzman for reading drafts, offering feedback, talking through theoretical snarls, accompanying me on various island retreats, and buying me so much shit with dinosaurs on it.

And because talking about writing isn't the only way my community keeps me alive, love also to the folks who have fed me meals, talked to me on the phone, let me hug your babies and pet your kitties, knit me clothes, played D&D with me or just watched it over the internet together, and showed up for me in the thousand tiny ways that make up a life. Non-exhaustively, thank you to Cosette Derome, Jessie Ferne, and Vanessa Lakewood; to Holly-Kate Collinson-Shield, Nancy Fulton, Darren Kirk, Tara Newell, and Rachel Smith; to Jordan Dylan, Maria Lorenzi, and the rest of the Cousins; to Emma Rae Cawood, Jamie Dylan, and Wendy Wan; and to my family, who are very patient with the fact that I keep writing books about them. If I failed to thank you, I owe you a cookie.

Bibliography

Briggs, Laura, and Jodie I. Kelber-Kaye. "'There Is No Unauthorized Breeding in Jurassic Park': Gender and the Uses of Genetics." *NWSA Journal* 12, no. 3 (2000): 92–113. https://www.jstor.org/stable/4316764.

Cariou, Warren. "An Athabasca Story." *Lake: Journal of Arts and Environment* 7 (2012): 70–75.

Chude-Sokei, Louis. "The Uncanny History of Minstrels and Machines, 1835–1923." In *Burnt Cork: Traditions and Legacies of Blackface Minstrelsy*, ed. Stephen Johnson. Amherst: University of Massachusetts Press, 2012.

Creed, Barbara. *The Monstrous-Feminine: Film, Feminism, Psychoanalysis*. London and New York: Routledge, 1993.

DeTora, Lisa. "'Life Finds a Way': Monstrous Maternities and the Quantum Gaze in *Jurassic Park* and *The Thirteenth Warrior*." In *Situating the Feminist Gaze and Spectatorship in Postwar Cinema*, ed. Marcelline Block. Newcastle upon Tyne: Cambridge Scholars Publishing, 2008.

Interrupting Criminalization. *We Must Fight in Solidarity with Trans Youth: Drawing the Connections between Our Movements*. June 2022. https://www.interruptingcriminalization .com/solidarity-with-trans-youth.

Klinkenborg, Verlyn. "What Were Dinosaurs For?" *The New York Review*, December 19, 2019. https://www.nybooks.com/articles/2019/12/19/what-were-dinosaurs-for/.

Kriss, Sam. "Pale/ontology: The Dinosaurian Critique of Philosophy." *Full Stop*, April 22, 2015. https://www.full-stop.net/2015/04/22/features/sam-kriss/paleontology-the-dinosaurian -critique-of-philosophy/.

Macdonald, Helen. *H Is for Hawk*. Toronto: Penguin Canada, 2016.

Mulvey, Laura. "Visual Pleasure and Narrative Cinema." *Screen* 16, no. 3 (1975): 6–18. https://doi.org/10.1093/screen/16.3.6.

Piepzna-Samarsinha, Leah Lakshmi. "FEMME SHARK MANIFESTO!" Brown Star Girl, 2008. https://brownstargirl.org/femme-shark-manifesto/.

Pratt, E.J. *Towards the Last Spike*. Toronto: Macmillan, 1952.

Rieppel, Lukas. *Assembling the Dinosaur: Fossil Hunters, Tycoons, and the Making of a Spectacle.* Cambridge, Mass.: Harvard University Press, 2020.

Scott, F.R. "All the Spikes but the Last." In *The Collected Poems of F.R. Scott*, 194. Toronto: McClelland & Stewart, 1981.

Sharman, Zena. *The Care We Dream Of: Liberatory & Transformative Approaches to LGBTQ+ Health*. Vancouver: Arsenal Pulp Press, 2021.

TallBear, Kim. "A Sharpening of the Already Present: Apocalypse and Radical Hope." *Unsettle: Indigenous affairs, cultural politics, & (de)colonization* (Substack), October 11, 2022. https://kimtallbear.substack.com/p/a-sharpening-of-the-already-present.

Todd, Zoe. "Fossil Fuels and Fossil Kin: An Environmental Kin Study of Weaponised Fossil Kin and Alberta's So-Called 'Energy Resources Heritage.'" *Antipode: A Radical Journal of Geography* (November 2022). https://doi.org/10.1111/anti.12897.

Vider, Michelle. "If the Velociraptor from *Jurassic Park* Were Your Girlfriend." *The Toast*, April 27, 2015. https://the-toast.net/2015/04/27/if-the-velociraptor-from-jurassic-park-were-your-girlfriend.

Watters, Audrey. "The Tech 'Regrets' Industry." AudreyWatters.com, February 16, 2018. https://audreywatters.com/2018/02/16/the-regret-industry.

Yoshida, Emily. "Do Androids Dream of Colossal Women?" *Vulture*, October 21, 2017. https://www.vulture.com/2017/10/why-do-we-keep-putting-gigantic-naked-women-in-sci-fi.html.

Zimmerman, Jess. *Women and Other Monsters: Building a New Mythology*. Boston: Beacon Press, 2022.

Hannah McGregor is an academic, podcaster, and author living on the traditional and unceded territory of the Musqueam, Squamish, and Tsleil-Waututh First Nations. She is the director of publishing at Simon Fraser University, co-director of the Amplify Podcast Network, and co-founder of Witch, Please Productions, a feminist media company. Her previous books include *Refuse: CanLit in Ruins*, *A Sentimental Education*, and *Podcast or Perish*.